"*Shri Henkel has penned an insightful and thought-provoking look at the numerous challenges business professionals face every day. A quick read, full of indispensable advice, that should be required reading for every new manager.*"

— **Baron R. Birtcher**
Former CEO of a California-based real estate development firm, responsible for the management of over 400 employees

"*Each of the 365 mistakes clarifies exactly what new managers do wrong, and suggests ways to correct those mistakes before they get made. Since many technical managers struggle with people skills, this book should be on every new technical manager's desk.*"

— **James E. Gaskin**
Author/Consultant/Speaker
james@gaskin.com • 972-222-0900
Technology for small/medium businesses: www.networkworld.com/topics/smb.html

*"This book gives simple, basic and practical advice to new managers."*

> — Christy A. Zajack,
> SPHR, Executive VP, GWR
> www.globalworkresources.com

*"The author's knowledge is both expansive and insightful in terms of business management practices. This book provides practical and useful advice for managers at all levels of their career."*

> — **Peter I. Dworsky**, MPH, MICP
> Special Operations Coordinator
> Monmouth Ocean Hospital Service
> Corporation

# 365
# FOOLISH
# MISTAKES
## Smart Managers
## Make Every Day

# How and Why
# to Avoid Them

Shri L. Henkel

# 365 FOOLISH MISTAKES Sm
# Every Day How and Why to A

Copyright © 2006 by Atlantic Publishing Group, Inc.

1210 SW 23rd Place • Ocala, Florida 34474 • 800-814-1132 • 352-622-5836–Fax

Web site: www.atlantic-pub.com • E-mail sales@atlantic-pub.com

SAN Number :268-1250

ISBN-13: 978-0-910627-75-7 • ISBN-10: 910627-75-4

Library of Congress Cataloging-in-Publication Data

Henkel, Shri L., 1965-
  365 foolish mistakes smart managers make every day : how and why to avoid them / Shri L. Henkel.
       p. cm.
Includes bibliographical references and index.
ISBN 0-910627-75-4 (9780910627757)
  1. Management--Handbooks, manuals, etc. I. Title: Three hundred sixty-five foolish mistakes smart managers make every day. II. Title.

  HD38.15.H46 2006
  658.4--dc22
                           2006003670

EDITORS: Cheryl Morrissette • cheryl_morrissette@yahoo.com; Jackie Ness • jackie_ness@charter.net

GLOSSARY: Compiled by Christina Mohammed

COVER DESIGN, ART DIRECTION & INTERIOR DESIGN: Meg Buchner • megadesn@mchsi.com

Printed in the United States

# TABLE OF CONTENTS

## PART ONE: CONGRATULATIONS, YOU'RE A MANAGER! NOW WHAT?

## PART TWO: HONING YOUR SKILLS

## Chapter 15    Effective Meetings

## Chapter 16    Scheduling

# PART FIVE: THE "BIG THREE" TOPICS

## Chapter 17    Communication

## Chapter 18    Delegation

## Chapter 19    Motivation

## Glossary of Terms

# DEDICATION

*This book is dedicated to those first-time managers with clammy palms and the heart that skips a beat. I remember those days very well.*

*It's also dedicated to the business owners and managers whom I've worked with through the years. We learned a lot together and made the businesses better with our efforts.*

*Finally, this book is dedicated to my grandfather, John Henkel, who showed me the value of giving a full day's work to my employers and excelling in customer service to bring the customers back, and to my grandmother, Hannah Gum, who has worked hard her entire life and led the way for me to make my mark on the working world. I couldn't do it without these great examples.*

# FOREWORD

Scott Adams is the originator and cartoonist for the comic strip Dilbert. Possibly no other American satirist provides greater insight into the inner-workings of corporate life in America. Recently Scott Adams presented this situation: Wally, the project manager, comes to one of his subordinates asking about the status of "the RDI Project." Having no recollection what his superior is talking about and obviously something that has been casually thrown into the "C" drawer, the subordinate responds, "Am I working on that one?" In exasperation Wally responds, "You've been in charge of it for a year!" To which the project manager responds, "Oh, in that case, it's almost done." In the final window of the cartoon we see Wally is sitting in his office reflecting upon the conversation, thinking to himself: *half of being a manager is living with a vague feeling of uneasiness.*

The vague feeling of uneasiness characterizes the roles of most managers. Just like Wally, most manager have to plan the work, organize the work into a sensible plan of action, and then give it to someone else to do. But if the project fails, falls behind schedule, or looks like a tree planned by a committee , whose head do they come looking for? You got it – the manager. The buck stops there.

*365 Foolish Mistakes Smart Managers Make Every Day* is written to help managers recognize situations in the everyday work setting that may be a potential problem for them. Each section of the book addresses a separate management function with instructions given in a practical, "how-to-do" manner to help managers improve their skills in the position. Best of all, each section is supported and illustrated with actual real-life experiences from working managers in just about every management walk of life. As you read ahead, you may find yourself thinking: *You know, I had that very thing happen just last week.* Well, if that's the case, our job is done. Happy reading!

**Gerald K. Wells, Ph.D.;**
**Senior Associate, Bussey, Davis & Associates**

# INTRODUCTION

Being a first-time manager is exciting, but all first-time managers face many challenges. I created this book to help new managers learn the ropes, and I've tried to include a wide variety of the problems you will face. The table of contents will give you an idea of the topics we will discuss. Many sections of this book are written for departmental managers within businesses, but there is much information that will also help small-business managers.

We start with "Congratulations, You're a Manager! Now What?" That's how I felt the first time I was put in charge of a business. I was excited and scared at the same time. This section includes tips to help you get your feet wet in the management pool. I'll share ideas about what to expect and how to handle the initial problems and concerns you might encounter. When you become a manager, you will need to establish your authority. We'll review the good and bad ways to do this.

Once you are settled in, we will work on honing your skills, including your leadership and management skills. Then we will review ways to improve your effectiveness. There are things you can do to make your job easier while still gaining the respect of your boss and your employees. You may also be in a situation where you will need to interact with people in other departments. We'll talk about ways to make these situations better.

Your employees are a key to your success. As a manager you will probably be called on to interview, hire, and train new employees. The chance for you to handpick the people you will work with each day is a gift, and I'll help you learn to make effective choices and how to keep these people on your team. Once you hire and train the people you want, then you will need to manage them properly. Handling your people wrong will undo the good you did when you chose them. I'll share tips on how to deal with employees and how to maintain a good working relationship. Employees will respond better if you create a positive work environment; no one likes to work in a negative and dreary environment.

In all the years I've been a manager, I found three major topics that all managers need to understand and implement properly: communication, delegation, and motivation. We'll review how to communicate with, delegate to, and motivate your employees. This will be crucial to your success as a manager and in maintaining the handpicked team that you assembled.

You will encounter many issues and situations when you deal with various employees. No two employees are alike, and no two situations are exactly the same. We'll delve into how employees differ and how to handle those differences.

Periodically you will need to evaluate your employees. There are negative and positive ways to handle this. I'll share these tips with you. Sometimes employees don't do their jobs in a way that is beneficial for themselves or for the company. In these cases, you need to discipline them, and, occasionally, you have to fire them. This is one of the hardest things a manager must do; we'll review ways to handle these situations. You will need to conduct effective meetings with your team, and we'll discuss how to effectively schedule and reward employees.

Each chapter and section of this book will begin by giving you information about each subject, and then I will include various common mistakes that managers can make. Each mistake will have an explanation on what should be done differently. Reading this book will not eliminate all mistakes, but it will arm you with the information to fix many of the problems that you'll face.

On a final note, you may wonder why I feel qualified to write this book or why you should listen to anything I have to say on the matter. I'm proud to share my background with you. At the age of nineteen I managed my first business. I was the office manager in a land surveying office. It was a busy office and we maintained a steady stream of work. Soon after that, I got a job managing three busy departments in a large department store. This was a totally different atmosphere from managing an office, but it required many of the same skills along with an assortment of new abilities. A couple of years later, I became an assistant manager and worked my way up to managing a franchise pizza business. It was a challenge, but I learned a lot about effective hiring and personnel management.

My next position was to manage and reorganize a video store. This gave me the opportunity to acquire new skills and to use some of the other skills I had already learned. From here, I went to work at a local hospital and was promoted to a department manager. I spent a lot of time working with people in other departments and learned how to work together more effectively. After that, I was hired for a position in a chain furniture store where I worked with several different departments. A couple of years later, I managed a chiropractic office. This job utilized all of the skills I had acquired over the years. I also used all of my experience when I went to work with my brother in his contracting business. Now I work for myself, helping other business owners to streamline their businesses and to run them more effectively.

I hope that gives you an idea of the experience and background that I bring to this book and to you. Through the course of this book, I will also bring you real examples of things I tried that worked and I'll share things that didn't work. An effective manager can learn from the good things and the bad things.

Let's turn the page and dive into the world of management.

# PART ONE

# Congratulations, You're a Manager! Now What?

The idea of being a manager is exciting. Many people, especially new managers who worked their way up in the company, look forward to being in charge. It's a new experience, and you need to prepare for the challenges and rewards that are in front of you.

# CHAPTER 1

# New Manager— What's Next?

The idea of being a manager is exciting. Many people, especially new managers who worked their way up in the company, look forward to being in charge. It's a new experience, and you need to prepare for the challenges and rewards that are in front of you.

Many managers are concerned about how their employees will treat them. If you've worked together in the past, being the boss can be awkward. Any old resentment can be magnified by your new position. You should be prepared for the possibility of employees who will try to cause trouble for you—the new manager. Whatever their personal thoughts about your promotion, employees will be watching to see how you handle your new position. The commercial that said, "Never let them see you sweat" could apply here.

No one should expect you to be perfect from the beginning, but the employees will be watching while you settle in. Talk with your boss about the department and any positive and negative things he or she can share.

## MISTAKE #1
### I Should Talk with the Last Supervisor

This can work both ways. The former supervisor can share insightful information about the job, the employees, and your boss. But you should be careful about the information because it could be clouded. The former manager might have personal issues with people in the department and could give you biased information about them. Managers who feel that they were terminated unjustly might also give you biased information. You can talk with the person who is leaving, but consider the feedback carefully.

It could be helpful to review the latest evaluations for your team members. There is usually a place for them to enter comments and reactions. Be sure to check this section for the manager's thoughts and the employee's comments to get both sides of the story. You can make notes and discuss any particulars with the employee at a later time. I always kept a notebook with concerns, ideas, and suggestions about the job and the employees.

## MISTAKE #2
### I'll Keep My Notebook on My Desk So It's Handy

If you do have a notebook with details about the job and your employees, you must keep it in your locker or a locked drawer of your desk. No matter how innocent a thought or comment may be, it can be misconstrued. Save yourself the unnecessary headache by keeping the information out of the hands of others.

# START OFF ON THE RIGHT FOOT

It is so important to get off to a good start. I'll share some tips that will help you do that. We will delve into these points in more detail as you read through this book, but let's take a quick look at each point now.

## Ask Your Questions

You will have many questions about your new job. That is one reason to stay in touch with your boss — he or she can help answer these questions. You can also ask questions of the employees, but watch for wrong information.

> ### MISTAKE #3
> ### I Feel Like I Should Keep My Questions to Myself
>
> It is never good to keep important questions to yourself. When you don't know the answers, you aren't as effective as you could be. Ask questions and then implement the answers.

## Be Available to Your Employees

There are many times when a manager has a mountain of work on his or her desk that needs to get done, but managers still need to be available for their teams. Set time every day to work with your team and to be available. When an employee asks you for help, you need to be there. If you are busy, let the employee know that you will be available soon. Remember to find him or her and offer your help when you're free. This means a lot to your team and makes your job easier.

## MISTAKE #4
### I Need to Stay in My Office or Behind My Desk to Finish My Work

Do the necessary work at your desk or in your office, but then get out and be available to your team. You are a manager, and that requires you to manage the people on your team. That is very difficult with an office or desk always separating you. It is better to be a hands-on manager.

## Be Confident, Not Cocky

Your team needs to see that you are confident in your ability to do the job. Show your employees that you are confident, but not arrogant. You will have some faults, but these make you human. You need to find the answers to your questions and ways to overcome your shortcomings without losing confidence in your abilities.

## MISTAKE #5
### My Employees Will Understand That I "Know It All"

You don't like a "know it all" any more than your team members do. That attitude is even more irritating from a new manager who can't possibly know everything. Be honest that you don't know everything and it will take time to learn everything the job entails. They will appreciate your honesty.

## Be True to Yourself

It won't do you any good to pretend to be someone or something that you are not. All sorts of people will give you advice on how to do your job. It's good to listen, but use your own judgment about what you should and shouldn't do.

## Take It Slow

It takes time for anyone to settle into a new job. I've found its better to move slower and do a thorough job from the beginning. Too many managers try to attack everything at once; no one can do that effectively. A friend recently took on a management job and has only been with the company for a few weeks. She doesn't know the people involved and what has worked in the past, so the ideas she tosses out have limited effectiveness. It would be much more effective for her to learn about the people and the company first.

---

### MISTAKE #6
#### I Have to Do Everything Right Away

When people rush into the unknown, they tend to make more mistakes. In your new position as a manager, that attitude will hurt you. Learn the job one step at a time, and earn the respect of your employees as you learn and become more effective.

---

## Listen to Your Boss and Employees

Your boss knows it's in his or her interest to help you learn your job. I had one boss who didn't feel this way, and it caused difficulties for six months. That was the exception in my experience. When your boss calls you or sends a memo, take the time to read it and try to learn from it. You should let your boss know if you don't understand something and put his or her suggestions into practice. Your employees can also share useful information with you, but until you get to know them, it's good to be cautious about the information they share with you.

### Stay in Touch with Your Boss

Communicate with your boss. He or she is your lifeline to the information and help you will need. If you encounter problems with your boss, they need to be addressed right away to keep the lines of communication open.

### Be Honest and Upfront with Your Employees

Once the initial cold feet warm up, you should call a meeting with your team. Let them know that they will continue to do their jobs the same as before. Tell them that you are coming into the position with an open mind and you want to learn more about the business. Encourage cooperation and open communication by being approachable. It's a lot to cover, but the team members need to hear this from you in the beginning.

---

## MISTAKE #7
### I Should Make Big Changes Right Away

Chances are that you won't need to make any big changes within the business or department that you manage. Even if changes are needed, they aren't your first priority. Get to know the people and the business first. This knowledge will enable you to make informed changes; changes based on reliable information are more effective.

---

## LEARNING THE ROPES

As a manager, you will need to keep your boss and your employees happy. Each decision has at least two possible outcomes, and you need to find the best solutions. Rest assured that making decisions will become easier as you gain experience, although people will expect you to find the answers quicker. You need to be patient about your abilities and take the time to learn the job responsibilities. If you are unsure about how to handle something, ok consult your boss.

## MISTAKE #8
### It Would Be Easier on Me to Learn Slowly

Put sufficient effort into learning your new job. There is a lot to learn, but you must work hard to learn your responsibilities. Your boss and team members will notice if you don't make progress in your job. Your boss will give you time, but don't abuse that patience and cause problems by taking too long to learn what is required of you as a manager.

When you evaluate a situation, remember that appearances can be deceiving, and get all the facts before you make a decision. Quick and accurate decisions will become easier once you get to know more about the business, the products or services that are offered, and details about the individual employees.

## MISTAKE #9
### I Make Decisions Without All the Details to Save Time

Don't make decisions without getting the facts. Jumping to conclusions can cause many problems. Your employees won't trust you to help with problems, and they may not bring problems to you if you don't give them the amount of thought that you should.

A manager has influence on the behavior and work of his or her employees. When you want your employees to do quality work, you need to lead them with quality work. You need to give your team proof that you have the skills to do the job.

## MISTAKE #10
### I Think I'll Pick the Office Gossip as a Mentor

You need to pick a potential mentor carefully. A person who wants to share the employee secrets is not the person you need. Find a person who will provide productive and helpful information to help you learn your responsibilities.

Who within the business or your department could serve as your mentor? He or she could be someone who worked the job in the past or a long-time employee of the company. You might want to ask your boss if he or she could suggest someone who you can trust to work with you.

One of the most important qualities in a manager is the ability to listen. That includes listening to your boss and your employees. You have responsibilities to all of these people. When they speak, you need to listen to what they have to say. Listen to all sides of the story. There is more than one side to everything. When you are confronted with a new situation, you need to ask questions.

You will develop the ability to ask the right questions. There is a real skill to asking effective questions that get the information that you want or need to make accurate decision. Listening to your employees will give you a better idea of the questions to ask. Then you need to listen to their answers.

Take some time to review the rules and regulations for the job. There may be a training manual or a specific manual for your job. Ask your boss if you can see any procedures, regulations, reports, and other memos to help you learn and understand more about the business and its products and services.

> ### MISTAKE #11
> ### *I'll Stare at the Beautiful Woman at the Desk*
>
> When you take time to watch what goes on in your department, casually glance at the people. It's easy to stare and leer, but it won't help your reputation. It could also start a lot of problems. Be casual and do not stare.

During your first days, it's good to watch what's going on around you. This will help you gather information about who is working, who spends time on the phone, who takes a lot of breaks, and who spends excessive time talking instead of working. You can also notice who works hard and which people appear to be productive. All of these insights will broaden your knowledge of your department.

## PHASING OUT THE ACTING SUPERVISOR

This can be a delicate situation depending on how the acting supervisor feels about you and your new job. Did the acting supervisor want your promotion? That is a detail that you need to know, because it could make things difficult for you. It wouldn't change whether you take the job or not, but it will help you to be armed and ready for potential problems. If the acting supervisor wanted the job, then he or she may be resentful.

I dealt with this in one job. A co-worker was convinced that she deserved the job and was very unhappy that I was promoted. She offered to help me, but then caused problems with the employees behind my back. I was suspicious when she congratulated me about the promotion and then complained to a long-time friend in another department. He confirmed my suspicions. To defuse the situation, I scheduled this employee for another shift that I knew she really liked, thus limiting our interaction.

It's possible the acting supervisor was only helping while the boss searched for a replacement. If he or she didn't want the job permanently, it will be much easier for you. In this situation, the acting supervisor should support you and help to transition the employees through the management change..

---

### MISTAKE #12
#### My Team Shouldn't Talk to the Acting Supervisor

If handled right, this transition will end quickly. When you overreact, it makes you look insecure. This isn't the impression you should give your team this early in your job.

---

Your new employees may be slow to acknowledge that you are in charge. This could be because they are familiar with the acting supervisor and it's easier to talk with someone they already know. Continue to prove that you are in charge and you want to help, and this situation should resolve itself.

If you continue to have problems with specific employees, you should talk with them in private. Remind them that you are the new manager and that you want to help them. Let them know that it is your responsibility to help them when there is a problem. Be patient for the first week or two and these problems should work themselves out. If this doesn't help, discuss the problem with your boss — but only after you have made reasonable attempts to solve the problem yourself.

When you replace another supervisor, there are additional factors that will affect the transition. Did the employees like or dislike the last supervisor? If they liked the last supervisor, it may take time to win them over. Don't let this get to you. Make every effort to show your team that you will work with them. They need to feel you have the best interests of the team in mind when you make decisions.

Was the last supervisor less than satisfactory? Were the employees happy to see him or her go? This sort of a situation makes it easier for you. Employees usually look for a manager who will make their situation easier to deal with and someone they can respect.

As you become more comfortable in your new position, work to build respect and a level of trust with your employees. It makes you more effective and makes it easier for you to do your job. Another good way to establish your credibility is to resolve personnel issues that bother the employees. This can be as simple as helping straighten out a bookkeeping error on their record or finding a way to rearrange part of the schedule. Start with small solutions, don't aim for sweeping changes.

## MISTAKE #13
### I Should Make Big Changes to Get Their Attention

This should seem logical, but many managers try to come in and change everything in the department or business. I've seen managers come into a business and insist on changing systems that already work well, just to make their mark. If there are business systems in place that work and the employees understand them, it would be better to leave them be.

My name is Allison Knight and I am a published author. The road to publication is full of possible potholes and obstacles. This is just one of the many lessons I learned along the way. After the sale of three books to a publisher, we submitted a fourth. According to the contract, they were to reply in 60 days. When they did not, my agent sent a terse letter asking for the proposal return.

It took years before that company bought another book from us.

**Lesson learned:** Take time to investigate and fully understand company procedures.

Allison Knight, Author
**www.allisonknight.com**

# CHAPTER 2

# First-Time Managers

**Y**ou have learned some of the initial problems that face a first-time manager. Now we need to delve deeper into what's involved in your job and what you should expect. Facets of your job will change, and you need to be prepared. How can you have successful working relationships with your boss and employees? Let's talk about how you can define your role as a manager.

## DEFINE YOUR ROLE

In your new position, you will be supervising a number of people. The person who hired you felt you were qualified for the added responsibility. Were you successful in your last position? In order to be successful as a manager, you must excel in different ways.

## MISTAKE #14
### The Business Situations Only Involve Me

When you are faced with a problem in your new job, you need to solve the problem in a way that will benefit the group. The team is your responsibility; they will look to you for a cooperative and team-oriented answer to problems.

Motivating your employees will help them excel in their jobs. There are various personalities that need to be blended within your team. Before, you only needed to motivate yourself, but now you're responsible for the entire team. Their performance is a reflection on you.

There are two very distinct management styles. One way is quiet and subtle while the other is loud and pushy. The loud and pushy style can make employees feel like they have been beaten over the head. This is a management style that gets short-term results but does not work in the long term. People who respond to this style are motivated by fear and intimidation. When employees feel threatened, they don't do their best work.

## MISTAKE #15
### I've Been Told to Intimidate My Employees

I had an assistant manager who will be a great example for various issues in this book. He barked orders at the employees who worked his shifts. He didn't act that way on my shifts, but he tried to intimidate them when I was gone. When he asked the employees to do anything, they grumbled and only did part of the task. On my shifts, they did what I asked and more. I worked as hard as anyone, and they respected that. We all worked hard together on my shifts and we all went home exhausted, but we did a good job. They told me that our shifts together were exhausting but satisfying.

A more effective management style is subtle and quiet. This is a great way to earn your employees' respect. You can still direct the employee activities with a quiet style. They will learn to work with you and cooperate because they support you. This is a wonderful way to gain long-term results from your team.

---

### MISTAKE #16
### *My Team Is Doing Well; I Can Shirk Some Duties*

The example above showed a manager who would slack off and shirk his duties. When you lead by example, the employees respond and do a much better job. If you expect your employees to work hard, then you'll have to work hard too.

---

The most effective way to get cooperation and respect from your employees is to lead by example. Motivated and hard-working employees don't want to be overseen by a manager who does not lead by example. This management style makes you more effective and makes your employees work harder, which makes you look better. Everyone in your department or business will be happier, including your boss.


## WHAT SHOULD YOU EXPECT?

When you become a manager, you should expect changes in your personal life and in your business life. A new manager can be overwhelmed by the new responsibilities and will find it hard to balance everything that needs to be done. I'll include some ideas and suggestions to help you manage your personal and professional responsibilities.

## MISTAKE #17
### I Feel Like I'll Never Get All My Work Done

It is possible to get all the work done. You need to find a system that works for you. It's easier to focus on paperwork and scheduling when you aren't interrupted with questions. Sometimes it's good to come in early or stay late. I used to have to work on holidays at one job because we had minimal staff. Because they didn't want to be stuck at work all day, the employees got the job done as quickly as possible.

You need to use your time well. Prioritizing your responsibilities is something we will discuss throughout this book, and this is definitely a time when you should prioritize. Managers usually go to work before their employees and work late into the evening. This will put a strain on your personal life. It's something that you need to discuss with your family and friends before you start the job, if possible, but it's never too late to talk with them.

Various things will be affected by your job as a manager, including your family and friends, where you spend time, your pay and expenses, your energy level and health, your free time, clubs, activities, and your lifestyle. Your stress level will also increase.

You need your family to be supportive, understanding, and fair in the ways they deal with you. Your new responsibilities will put more pressure on you, and their support will be invaluable. Without their support, your stress level will be even higher and take a bigger toll on your mental and physical health. No matter what you may think, you don't have unlimited time and energy. Discuss the pros and cons of your decision with your family, and formulate a plan to adjust to your promotion.

## MISTAKE #18
### My Personal Life Can Stay the Same

When you become a manager, your life will change. Your family cannot expect things to stay the same. Many spouses have a problem with the new schedule. Each promotion requires some adjustments, and management jobs are no different. Managers make more money and, in turn, the company demands more from them. I've had many jobs in management and only one didn't increase my work hours. That supervisor wouldn't allow anyone to have overtime, so I had to get everything done in 40 hours each week. It was exhausting, and I worked a lot of unpaid weekends and holidays to get everything done.

Even though you are busier than ever, you need to save time for your hobbies and interests. You need this downtime and the renewal that these activities provide. Whether you are single or married, an effective manager needs at least one trusting and sharing individual in his or her life. These things help you maintain balance in your life, which enables you to be more effective in your job and happier in your personal life.

## BASIC FUNCTIONS OF A MANAGER

Are you apprehensive about managing a group of people for the first time? It can be a little unsettling, but we'll prepare you for the challenges that lie ahead. I don't want to overwhelm you, but remember that there will also be phone calls and pages, along with other interruptions and mountains of paperwork. Our next priority is to help you deal with all of these things.

### Giving Instruction to Employees

## MISTAKE #19
### Some of My Employees Are Better Than Others

You need to avoid saying anything that could be misconstrued to mean one employee is better than another. Even if you believe this, you shouldn't tell the employees who are involved. Express your confidence in their abilities equally.

You need to encourage your team members. Be careful how you word these comments. Tell employees that you have confidence in their ability. Suggest that they try some new ways of doing the job. When you give direction, do this firmly. Let employees know what they need to do, and give them additional directions when they need them.

## MISTAKE #20
### They Don't Respond; I Need to Be More Bossy

It's easy to get frustrated. I remember many times when things were crazy and one employee couldn't understand the instructions I was giving. When you see a blank look, you can tell that an employee doesn't understand what you're saying. It's difficult, but you must maintain a calm exterior. If you give voice to your frustration, it will take even longer to explain the information.

### Attire

This can be complicated in the beginning. Some businesses have a definite dress code while others allow various outfits and styles. If you are in a business that requires a uniform, then the decision is made for you. However, you may have a situation where some people wear jeans while others may dress more professionally.

## MISTAKE #21
### I'll Wear Jeans Since I Saw a Manager in Jeans

It's always better to dress up instead of down to avoid making a bad impression. If your attire wasn't discussed during the interview process, then wear something dressier; you can always dress down another day. You can also remove a tie and dress jacket if you later find the dress code is casual.

Along this same line of thought, have you noticed the way people dress is often an indication of the type of work they do? Here are some examples:

- A banker—Suit and tie, dress suit or nice dress.

- A chef or cook—Casual with a white apron and a hat or hair net.

- A mechanic—Jeans and T-shirt, usually with grease on clothes.

These are just a few examples, but clothing really does make the man or woman. Once you get on the job, if your boss says you can dress more casually, then dress down. It would be better to overdress until you can verify the company policy.

### Your Management Style

What is management style? This becomes an issue when you need to decide how hands-on to be. In some jobs, you will give assignments and the employees will do their jobs. Other situations require more supervision because of company policy or outside factors and rules. These things will determine what type of management style you need for your job.

If you decide to delegate work, you will have a more hands-off approach to your job. (There are many positive and negative aspects to delegating that we'll talk about in Part Four.) This style needs qualified people who know their jobs. You also need to be within a company that allows the freedom to do the job with fewer restrictions. The hands-on approach will take more of your time and effort, but the company you work for may insist on that style.

## MISTAKE #22
### I'll Watch My Employees Closely Whether They Need Me or Not

This isn't a productive approach. If the company gives employees the freedom to do the job, and you learn they don't need to be watched, then don't hover. Many people cannot work with someone watching them, and you could cause unnecessary problems.

### Is There a Perfect Management Style?

One management style will not work for every situation. There are many variables that affect which management style you need. Your style needs to be a mix that complements your personal style, your employees' personalities, and what the company requires.

You must address the differences in your employees. Some will work on their own, requiring little supervision. Other employees cannot get the job done without direction. You must determine which employees need your attention and which don't. Differences don't make one employee better than another; they just make them different.

## MISTAKE #23
### I'll Create One Management Style for Everyone

This is the wrong approach. You could give needy employees too little assistance and smother employees who don't need your constant attention. Treat each employee as an individual with various needs.

### Instruction and Follow up with Employees

When you give instructions, be clear. It's better not to ramble about unimportant things when you give instructions. The way you give instructions will depend on the project and the person you are helping. Some employees need a lot of details while others only need specifics. I've worked with some employees who needed detailed instructions, including a drawing or sketch to help them visualize what I wanted. Other employees would be bored and resentful if they were given that many details.

## MISTAKE #24
### Maybe I Should Be More Forceful with Details

When you give instructions about a project, you need to give enough details to be clear, but don't talk "down" to the person. Never talk to the employee in a degrading way.

Directions should be given to the employee one-on-one. This can be done in a meeting if there are general instructions. Employees who are involved in more complicated projects should be talked to one on one about the additional information. This is also true for unusual projects. Use your common sense and experience to determine which assignments need more instruction.

After a reasonable amount of time, follow up with employees to see how the project is progressing. Unless the team member is self-sufficient, it's good to check in at least once a day. Check with the employees to head off potential problems. They may not feel comfortable asking questions, and that will delay their completion of the task.

## MISTAKE #25
### None of My Employees Need to Be Overseen

This is a dangerous approach. It's unlikely that your employees won't need any oversight. Remember, the work your employees do will reflect on you. If they don't complete the work or if they don't do the work right, it will reflect on you as a manager.

There are several factors that will influence how much follow up you need on the instructions you gave. An easier project needs less follow up, while complicated projects should require more follow up. The abilities of the employee will also dictate how much follow up is needed. When you talk to employees, it's good to ask them about the project casually. You might want to ask about something that you know they are interested in and then ask about how the project is going. Another possibility is to ask if they have any questions or concerns.

Your boss will also affect how often you follow up. If your boss is pushing you, then you will probably check on projects more often.

### *Your Paperwork Jungle*

All managers have paperwork to deal with, so they need to learn to handle it. We would all love to see it disappear, but I don't think it ever will. Most managers are told that they have to take care of all paperwork every day. This is an unreasonable expectation, and there is a better way.

Here is an approach that will help you maintain the deluge of paper:

1. Identify what papers are the most critical. Some things will not wait, and those are the papers that must be dealt with every day.

2. Make a separate pile of things that need to be handled within a day or two, and be sure to review those in short order.

3. You will receive memos and reports that you can read and then forward to another department. Do this quickly to get that paper off your desk.

4. Create files for reports, memos, etc., that you need to keep in your personal file, so that you can refer to them in the future.

5. Last are the memos. Many are unimportant; you can scan those and discard them (be sure they are not important before you toss them).

## MISTAKE #26
### *I Don't Need a Plan for My Paperwork*

Many managers have ways to handle the inevitable paperwork. The suggestions listed above are simple and would be easy to implement. You may not believe it in the beginning, but you will have a mountain of paperwork to deal with on a daily or weekly basis.

In a complex manufacturing system, the best detail techy was made the group manager over engineers, supervisors, and shift workers. His instinct was to bury himself in the myriad data detail generated each day. Any conflict, management, or relational issues were simply out of his purview because he stayed buried in the technical details. Even in site staff meetings, he always had a stack of data he was working on.

The result was a kind of impromptu team at the level below him, but some issues had to go to his desk. That mostly resulted in frustration on all sides.

It clearly demonstrated that some management interests and skills need to accompany the great tech skills for the group leader to be effective.

Hill Kemp, Author
**www.capitoloffense.com**

# CHAPTER 3

# What Managers Need to Know

## DEALING WITH TOUGH SITUATIONS

Every manager will face "panic button" situations. This is a normal part of the job, so every effective manager needs to learn how to deal with tough situations.

### MISTAKE #27
#### I Don't Think I Can Handle Problem Situations

Even if the task seems impossible in the beginning, you shouldn't tell your boss it is impossible. Ask your boss questions about what he or she needs. Keep a positive attitude, and gently push for complete answers to your questions. Your boss will respect you because you are willing to take on a challenge.

## Rush Projects

There will be times when your boss will come to you with a rush job. Maybe it's a project that would normally take a couple of weeks, but your boss needs it to be completed within a few days. There can be many reasons for the urgency, but it's probably something your boss couldn't control. It's best to dig in and prepare a plan of action.

### MISTAKE #28
#### I Don't Think I Can Stay Calm with This Deadline

Even if you are worried and concerned about an assignment, you need to stay calm in front of your employees. If you panic, they will think it's all right for them to panic. That can cause problems and delay the project while you calm the team. Do everything possible not to show your concern; you'll impress your boss and put your employees at ease.

These situations happen from time to time, so you need to be prepared when they do. Your boss and employees will watch to see how you will react. Show them that you can handle the pressure.

Many managers will run in circles before they absorb what needs to be done. This kind of scattered and panicked reaction isn't what your boss wants to see from you. A cooler and calmer mind will help you make progress. Here are some tips to help you get a handle on a rush project:

### Identify What You Need to Do

Take a deep breath and find out what is needed. In a small company, the orders probably only go through one or two people before they reach you. However, if you are in a large company, the orders might be relayed through a large number of people.

Do you remember the "gossip" game from when you were a child? One person said something and then each person told another person. When the gossip got to the other side of the room, the comment had changed dramatically. This same thing can happen with directions in a company. It is even worse when there is a rush. You could easily miss some of the details.

### Determine the Details

Once you have a general idea of what you need to be working on, you need to make sure you have all of the details. There are some things that you need to verify in the beginning. Verify the payroll and overtime that can be spent. If you spend too much, it will cause big problems for you in some situations. Determine if you can bring in help from other sources or other departments. It is good to list any additional help you need and distribute this information to your boss and others who will be involved.

## MISTAKE #29
### I'm Sure I Have All the Facts from My Boss

Your boss may come to you in a panic about a rush project. He or she will give you the details in a shotgun style. The facts may be scattered, and you might not have all of the details. It's in your best interest to review the information with your boss in a calm setting, asking plenty of questions. Make sure you feel comfortable about the specifics before you start the project.

When you discuss the project with your supervisor, you should make notes about all the specifics and ask any questions you have about the job. At that point you should be ready to start working on the project. It's a good idea to create a memo with the details as you understand them and send it to your boss. If you talk to other supervisors, send a copy of the memo to them as well. Don't contact other supervisors unless you know it's acceptable — you might end up causing trouble for your boss. Having the facts in writing will protect you if there is a problem or a misunderstanding.

### MISTAKE #30
### I Think I Have All the Information and Help I Need

When you ask for information or people for a project, question your boss if you don't get what you requested. If you need the supplies or people, then make sure you get them. There is the possibility your boss is testing you to make sure that you can succeed. Another possibility is that your request could've been misplaced.

When you request specific help and it isn't given to you, those concerns need to be mentioned to your boss. You need to contact outside sources that will supply materials, people, or anything else you need. Let them know in writing that you must be notified immediately if there's a problem getting the resources you requested. Inform your boss about any significant delays right away. If you can resolve the delay, then don't bother your boss.

### Follow Up and Keep an Eye on the Progress
As the manager, you need to stay on top of the progress for your project. This enables you to give accurate status reports when supervisors ask. Your prompt and accurate replies will show that you are managing the project well.

## MISTAKE #31
### My Team Doesn't Need Me to Follow Up

When you are responsible for a project, you need to follow up on a regular basis. For rush projects, you need to be involved in the project. It's easy for important details to be ignored if someone does not give them enough attention. You are that someone.

Be prepared that the supervisors above you will probably badger you about when the project will be done. They are just following up on you, so let them know that the project is on target and you will notify them as soon as it is complete. They know that asking you every couple of hours does not help it get done any more quickly, but they will probably do it anyway. Just remain calm and be respectful when they ask. When you encounter any significant progress or delays, these people should be notified and kept in touch.

### Ask Employees to Notify You of Problems

A way to avoid some rush situations and to help you get through others is to have your employees notify you when they notice potential problems. Some employees will come to you with small and trivial situations, but there will also be times when they notice legitimate concerns. Be patient when employees bring small things to your attention. Make them feel that they can approach you with all their concerns. Even when it's only a small problem, thank them for making the effort to tell you.

## MISTAKE #32
### It's Easier to Ignore Employee Problems

Even if it doesn't seem important, don't ignore employees when they come to you about problems. They are in a unique position to let you know about some problems. Listen and follow up on the information they bring to you.

Some problems that employees might notice before you would notice them include equipment malfunctions, supply shortages, distribution problems, price increases, employee shortages, missing documents, late deliveries, and insufficient details. If certain employees approach you repeatedly about trivial issues, thank them for their help and then give them some additional details about the sort of information that you really need. There will always be people who will come to you about unnecessary things, but thank them for trying to help.

### Finish the Project on Time

When your team finishes the project, send it to the people who need it. Then you can take a breath and thank each person who worked to help you reach this goal. When you receive recognition for a job well done, pass this on to the people who helped you.

You should also let the supervisors know that your employees were a big part of your success. It's wonderful if you can tell your supervisors this in front of the employees. You need to show your appreciation to your team members. Don't underestimate how much they will appreciate recognition for a job well done. Do you remember how you felt before you were a supervisor? Did you appreciate it when your manager took credit for your work? Of course not, and your team won't appreciate it either.

### MISTAKE #33
#### I'm the Manager, So I Deserve the Credit

When your boss or other supervisors congratulate you on a job well done, share that recognition with the employees who helped you. This will build their respect for you and make them more willing to help you on another project.

## Recurring Projects

Take the time to review your job duties to see if there are any projects that are recurring each month. Some of these might include end-of-the-month reports, meetings about reaching quotas, inventory reports, placing orders, or payroll specifics. You know each of these things happen every month. Many happen at the beginning or end of each month. Can you find a way to adjust your schedule to make these recurring duties less stressful for you and your department?

### MISTAKE #34
#### Some Things Happen Every Month and Will Always Be a Problem for Me

There are many problems that you can make better with a little effort and creativity. When you are faced with a recurring problem, evaluate it and see if there is a way you can make it easier.

One simple task that I had in one of my management jobs was to figure the food orders for the following week. This may not seem difficult, but I had to take a lot of things into account in order to do it right. First, I had to maintain my food budget. Next, I had to review any special events that week. We catered to a large college campus, so events had a huge impact on how much food we needed. I also had to be familiar with the usual items we needed to ensure that we would have enough of those things. Another consideration was that many products would spoil quickly.

Each of those factors was figured into my order. If I made mistakes, it would affect the monthly profit and loss statement, along with my monthly bonus. So I set aside extra time earlier in the week to talk with people who knew about upcoming student and campus events, and they helped me figure what I needed before the order deadline. This is a simple example, but it shows that planning ahead can save unnecessary hassles at the last minute.

Can you work on these recurring tasks ahead of time? Maybe you could compile numbers or start making lists early. Then you could update with data for the last days of the month. Only you can look at your projects and see if some work can be done early.

### Learning from a Crisis

Take time to evaluate a particular situation and figure out ways to prevent the things that caused the problem. To follow are some questions that you might want to ask yourself. Do the answers provide some ideas on how to head off major problems?

- Can we be prepared if the same thing happens again?

- How can I prepare myself to handle this problem in the future?

- Who would I need outside my team to make this work better?

- What do we need to keep this from happening again?

- Is there a better way to tackle problems?

- Is something specific causing the problems that can be changed?

- Am I overreacting to the situation?

- If similar problems creep up periodically, can I handle them better?

Evaluate repetitive situations to develop a system to be better prepared. Discuss the situations with key members of your team to see if you can prepare better for these problems. Finding ways to handle them better will help your entire team. If you approach it from that angle, your team members can see the benefit to finding solutions.

It is important to maintain a full staff during your "crunch times." Determine when you have important deadlines, and mark these on the calendar. This allows you to make sure there are enough staff members to meet the deadlines. If there is a particularly tight deadline, you might eliminate any vacations until the project is complete. That's better than telling an employee at the last minute that they cannot have time off.

## MISTAKE #35
### I Promised an Employee Vacation Time, but Now We Are in a Crunch

After you create a schedule around your crunch times, check it before you approve vacations. If there is a critical project to be done, all employees need to be available.

If you create the appearance of a crisis unnecessarily, it causes undue stress for you and others in your department. You can also cause problems for yourself by doing this. Your boss could see this as a way to get attention or to gain recognition for solving a problem that never existed. None of this is good for    you in the long run, so don't blow a situation out of proportion.

## MISTAKE #36
### I'll Ignore My Boss; He's Overreacting Again

You may realize your boss is overreacting to a situation. Even if you know it's not a crisis, don't belittle your boss's concerns. Your calm reply should help, but respect his or her opinions and help resolve the situation.

Keep in mind that some people will see everything as a crisis. When you remain calm, it can help the other person calm down. Two people overreacting to a problem doesn't make it better.

## MISTAKE #37
### I Can Overreact Since My Boss Does

It will not help to have two people overreact; try to remain calm. Your team members need to see your calm reaction, but don't downplay something that is critical. It can be a balancing act, but it will help you in the long run to handle it calmly.

# ESTABLISHING AN EFFECTIVE ROUTINE

In your initial weeks as a manager, you will probably feel you're being pulled in many directions at the same time. Actually, you are being pulled in opposite directions. Your boss pulls you in one direction by giving you assignments. At the same time, your employees pull you in another direction with their questions and needs. When you are the "new guy," there are so many new names and faces to keep straight. At the same time, paperwork is piling up on your desk.

You will soon find that you must focus on multiple projects at the same time while dealing with a steady stream of distractions. It can be overwhelming to learn the various elements of your job.

When you develop a daily routine, it will help you get control of your duties. You need to establish a routine that will work for you and your team, keeping your personal abilities and limitations in mind. Your energy level is another important issue that must be considered.

Everyone works better during certain times of the day than during others. Determine when you are more productive and build your routine around those restrictions. Utilize your best time of day to tackle the toughest projects. For instance, morning people should schedule their harder tasks in the morning. You still have to work a full day, but planning your workload based on your natural rhythms helps you get the most work done and mold your routine to your strengths and weaknesses.

Are you a person who has a hard time starting projects? This can be a problem for a manager. You must be able to start projects and then see them through to completion. The best way for some people to get started is to dive right in. Others need to take time to plot and plan what they will do and then find ways to involve their team members.

The amount of time you have available will affect the approach that is needed. If you have a tight deadline, then you'll have a limited amount of time to start the project. You will become better at organizing and executing projects as you get more experience.

Managers need to schedule some quiet time to plan. If you have an office, you can work there, but be careful about closing yourself off from your staff; this will put a barrier between you and your team. It is better if you leave the door open so that you are still accessible to your employees. When you plan, remember that all plans must be flexible. Every day will be unpredictable, and you need to adjust to whatever the day brings.

I have my own communications company. I've been in business for one and a half years. One mistake I made in the past year is not setting clear enough parameters for people I subcontract to. One subcontractor took much longer to write some articles and proposals than I thought she would, and it resulted in a cost overrun for the whole job. The job was already firmly quoted, so it meant I got paid less in the end.

I have found a way around this. I figured out how much each component of the job will take and how much I get paid, as well as how much each subcontractor gets paid. Now I know how long I can spend on the job and still make money, and I will give the subcontractor a set fee for her part of the job (she can raise her pay by working more quickly).

Sandra Reimer, Writer/Publicist
Reimer Reason Communications
sandra@reimer-reason.ca

When I began my company five years ago, I was very excited about being a manager. I could boss people around. I was in charge. I jumped right in and found people to do all the things I did not have time to do and I told them what I needed to be done.

Eventually I found myself overwhelmed with projects and a group of people doing nothing because I had not taken any steps to manage or lead them. I did not follow up with them, I did not give them any instruction, and I did not give them any support as a manager. I did, however, complain when things did not get done.

I can't stress enough how important communication is when managing any size group. I recently purchased a Franklin Covey system and I am learning the fine art of lists and priorities. I make a list of tasks that need to be completed, who needs to complete them, and by when. I have an initial conversation with whoever receives that task, and then I plan follow-ups to ensure progress is being made. Finally, I make that final project contact with thanks and praise for a job well done.

Karen L. Syed, President
Echelon Press Publishing
**www.echelonpress.com**

# CHAPTER 4

# Establish Authority

## HOW TO ESTABLISH YOUR AUTHORITY

Different people exercise their authority in different ways. Some managers are mild mannered, while others are rude and blustery. Being rude is not the answer when you deal with others. You need to find a better way to establish your authority.

### MISTAKE #38
#### A Friend Said I Should Be Rude to My Employees

Harsh, rude, and blustery managers are not effective. They may get short-term results driven by fear, but they aren't effective in the long term. You will start out better with your team members when you treat them with respect.

To firmly establish your authority, you will have to do several things. One big grandstand event won't be enough. Since you are the new manager, the employees will watch you. Don't look like you're filled with doubt. Show your employees that you make you're own decisions.

## MISTAKE #39
### I Would Like to Let Someone Else Make Decisions

It is especially critical in your early days as a manager to make your own decisions. If you let others make decisions, you'll send negative signals to your employees. Ask for help if you need it, but don't ask others to do your job.

In the beginning, encourage employees to bring their questions to you. Once you understand the job, let the employees make some of the routine decisions. You need to set limits for how much they can decide without your input.

Not only do you need to make more decisions when you begin a new management position, you also need to be more hands-on. This will help you learn the responsibilities and qualifications of your employees. Once you understand the department or business dynamics, you are better qualified to decide who needs more supervision and who can work on their own.

## MISTAKE #40
### I'm New, So I'll Do Less with My Team Members

This is not an acceptable course of action. When you are a new manager, you need to work with your employees. This helps them get to know you and it helps you learn to do your job. Once you are established, you can decide which decisions you should make yourself and what you can delegate.

Do other supervisors expect you to manage like the last supervisor? They might want you to run the department in the same way, but you need to decide how to manage your team. You have to stand firm in your dealings with other managers.

When employees or other supervisors tell you the last manager did things a certain way, it's best to verify the information. Make sure they are telling you the truth before you spend time to considering the details. Be sure to make it clear that they cannot intimidate you and these people should back off.

When employees bring questions to you, do your best to answer them right away. Delays can be misconstrued to indicate that you don't care about your employees' concerns. Personnel issues are very critical to the employees who are involved. The quicker you resolve the problem, the more they will respect you. If there isn't a solution, you need to determine that soon and explain the situation to them.

### MISTAKE #41
#### My Employees Have Concerns, But I Have Other Things to Do First

When employees come to you with problems, make them a priority. They came to you because they need help, and this is your opportunity to show they matter to you.

Answering employee questions quickly will help your new employees feel that they can come to you with problems and questions. They will also feel you care about them. By listening to and helping your employees, you'll quickly establish a more lasting kind of authority.

# HOW TO EARN YOUR EMPLOYEES' RESPECT

Employees who trust you will work harder for you, so it's in your best interest to gain their trust. This will not happen overnight, but there are ways to help them respect and trust you in a timely manner. The following tips will help you gain your employees' respect.

## MISTAKE #42
### I'm a Manager; I Should Have Their Respect

Being promoted to a management position does not guarantee respect. You must earn respect, and this takes time and effort.

### Be Honest in Your Dealings

When you talk to your employees, you need to be honest and straightforward—even when the answer is bad news. In a company atmosphere, it is amazing how quickly rumors spread. It is imperative that you be honest from the beginning. When you learn details about a project, talk with the employees that are affected.

### Ask Employees for Their Input

This will show the employees that you trust them and want to hear what they have to say. You don't have to agree with everything they say, but your employees will respect you when you ask for their input.

### Show Appreciation

There are many times employees do things that help you. These can be simple things or supporting you in a big project. When employees help you, show your appreciation. Even though you are the manager, they don't owe you. Give them credit when it is due.

### Pay Attention to Their Concerns

In the beginning you will probably hear a lot about employees' concerns. People tend to recycle their old complaints when there's a new manager. It's a fresh opportunity for them to find a solution. This is one of the things a new manager needs to deal with. Be sure to listen to what they are saying. These concerns can give you invaluable insights into the employees and the business.

### Look Out for the Interests of Your Department

There could be a chance that your department will be overlooked while you get established. In some businesses, the long-term managers have learned how to get favors for their departments. Since you're new, you don't know the tricks. If you notice there are real problems, you may need to talk with your boss.

### Don't Let People Goof Off

This goes against common sense, but you gain respect when you don't allow people to slack and goof off. When some employees goof off, other employees have to do their work. The people who are picking up the slack will appreciate that you are making the other people do their jobs.

## Some Employees Will Question Your Authority

As a manager, you will learn that it's difficult to handle people who question your authority. You were promoted, but that doesn't mean you will automatically get respect along with the job. Keep in mind that not all managers are questioned by their employees, but I want to include information on how to deal with it in case you have this problem. It may not even be a reflection on you. Many times, it is the nature of some employees who work on your team. You will find that most employees will give you the chance to prove yourself, but be prepared for the few who want to cause problems.

## MISTAKE #43
### I Resent That My Employees Hesitate to Trust Me

When employees hesitate to bring their questions to you in the beginning, you shouldn't assume this is an affront to you. Their hesitation could be concern about whether they can trust you. If they continue to avoid you after you make an effort to get to know them, then you might need to be concerned.

Some employees may have been mistreated by a past supervisor. That isn't your fault, but they might still be hesitant to trust you. Remember, your position gives you a certain power over your team members:

- You assign the tasks.

- You promote or demote employees.

- You give or deny raises to any team member.

- You hand out the discipline.

Each of these activities can make their life easier or more difficult, and your employees know that. They may want to take their time and get to know you before giving you their support. Once you prove that you won't criticize them, they will be more likely to share their problems and concerns.

## MISTAKE #44
### Employees Must Understand I'm In Charge

This attitude will not win their respect, but it will cause more problems. They understand that you are their manager, but you need to gain their respect, even if they question you at first.

Some employees will decide in the beginning that they don't trust you. They may choose to take their problems to your boss instead of you. In a perfect world, your boss should direct them to you. If he or she doesn't do this, it would be good for you to talk about the situation. Your employees need to understand that you're the manager and they need to come to you when they have questions.

## MISTAKE #45
### My Boss Knows the Employees Should Talk to Me

Your boss does know this, but sometimes people gravitate to the people they are familiar with. It doesn't hurt to remind your employees to bring problems and concerns to you.

When you determine that your boss is in agreement with you, then call the employee into your office for a talk. Let them know that you are the new manager and you want to be involved in everything that goes on in your department. This means that all problems and concerns need to be brought to you directly. They also need to learn that taking their concerns to others won't fix the problem.

Did an employee make negative or derogatory comments about you? If so, you need to discuss that with them. Draw him or her out and determine any underlying problem. Don't be harsh or rude, and don't lose your patience. Being irrational will only make the problem worse.

## MISTAKE #46
### Troublemakers Make Me So Mad That I Want to Tell Them What I Really Think

Even when employees upset you, it is critical to remain calm. Otherwise, they will know they succeeded in upsetting you. A harsh reaction will undermine your efforts and make you look bad to others in your department or business.

Keep an open mind when you talk with the employees. You may not agree with the way they handled their complaints, but is there any merit to their thoughts? When you sit back and consider what they said, it is possible that you could find ways to improve how you do your job.

## MISTAKE #47
### The Conversation Gave Them a Chance to Complain

When you have a problem with an employee, it's best to talk with them directly and privately to resolve the situation. They may mention specific things that bother them.

When your employees talk to you about their problems, they may try to convince you to do things in the same way that the previous manager did them. You don't have to try to do everything the same way, but you should listen to what your employees are saying.

## MISTAKE #48
### I Don't Care What the Last Manager Did

You don't have to make the same decisions the last manager made, but it won't hurt to consider the things they did. When you are a new manager, it is always good to get input from people who are familiar with the job and the business.

## Dealing With Employees Who Make You Look Bad

It's possible that one of your employees will make a conscious effort to make you look bad. Maybe an employee thinks that he or she should be the manager or was turned down for the position. Or, the person may just want to stir up trouble.

Here are some "red flag" actions that need your immediate attention. If your employees do any of these things, you need to address the situation right away.

- Do they correct you in front of others?

- Do they complain to others about you?

- Do they ask pointless questions to trip you up?

- Do they ask hard questions to embarrass you?

- Do they compare you to the previous supervisor?

- Do they challenge you in any way?

- Do they complain about how you treat them?

## MISTAKE #49
### It's Easier to Ignore This Behavior

It is easier, but you will end up with more problems. When you see these red flags in your department, you must deal with it right away. If you ignore the problems, they will grow, and more employees may model this unacceptable behavior.

Your employees may do other mischievous things, hoping to push your buttons. Keep in mind that the other employees and managers are watching how you will react. If you choose not to react, other troublemakers may step forward. Others will see that they can get away with causing trouble and join in. This could cause your other team members to doubt your ability to lead the group.

## MISTAKE #50
### When Employees Say Something Rude or Obnoxious, I Want to Be Rude to Them

Troublemakers say these things to get a reaction. When you don't get upset or lash out, they don't win. You need to stay in control when you deal with problem people.

When comments are made, you may ask the person to repeat the comment to make sure you heard it right. Some employees may talk behind your back, while the more obvious ones will make comments in front of you. The troublemakers may invite others to join in with them.

## MISTAKE #51
### I'm the Manager and I'll Straighten Them Out

When you have a problem with an employee, discuss it in private. This is not the sort of thing that should be talked about in a group setting. Also, protect yourself by making notes about your conversation. Write down what you said and how the employee responded.

When you take the employee aside, speak in private and make notes about the conversation. The situation could lead to disciplinary action, and your notes will be needed at that time. Remain calm while you talk, but be firm in your resolve. This employee needs to understand you are in charge and you won't put up with this sort of behavior.

When you talk with a difficult employee, you might mention the possibility of dismissal. This should indicate to the employee that you will not tolerate their actions. If they mention a transfer, you need to be careful. That would be the easiest solution, but that would make you look weak.

## MISTAKE #52
### An Employee Transfer Could Be a Good Solution

When you have problems with an employee, a transfer is not usually the best solution to your problem. Talk with the employee and explain why their behavior is not acceptable. They could be trying to get a transfer through their bad behavior. You would be rewarding them for being a problem. This is not a habit you want to start.

After your talk, the employee will either behave or will continue the bad behavior. As the manager, you can assign that employee the hardest or least desirable jobs. I know people who do this in an attempt to get the person to quit, but I would be careful about assigning all the bad jobs to one person. They could contend that you were singling them out and cause trouble for you. There is also the option to formally discipline them for their actions. Be sure to keep the notes from your earlier meetings to support the decision to discipline.

Brief your boss if the problem persists. He or she may have suggestions on how to handle the situation. Either way, your boss needs to be aware of the problem and be prepared if it escalates. You also need to notify your boss before you take any formal disciplinary action. This isn't a pleasant part of the manager's job, but it is necessary to handle it swiftly and with a firm hand.

# PART TWO

# Honing Your Skills

### Create Trust with Employees

*Creating trust with your employees is critical to long-term success as a manager. We've talked about the fact that you don't gain respect or trust overnight—you have to work on it. You need to manage in such a way that you will gain their trust.*

# CHAPTER 5

# Leadership Skills

I f you have a choice, would you do more for someone you trust or someone you don't trust? Most people would pick the person they trust. Chances are that your employees feel the same way.

## MISTAKE #53
### I'm Their Manager; Why Don't They Trust Me?

Have you given your employees any reason to trust you? This is an important question. If you haven't given them a reason to trust you, then they probably don't. You need to work on ways to earn their trust.

When you first walk into the department, your employees know nothing about you. Your actions will affect whether they can trust you. Let's talk about some things that you can do to help gain your employees' trust.

### Show That You Care

You want the trust and respect of your employees. That means you need to show that you respect them. You can show this by caring about them, and not just when they are at work. If they have a difficulty, then you need to help. This doesn't mean that you coddle them, but you do need to treat them with dignity.

---

## MISTAKE #54
### I'll Tell My Employees They Can Trust Me

That isn't good enough. You have to earn their trust and respect. You cannot issue a memo and expect to be trusted. This attitude will do more harm than good.

---

Sometimes it can be something as simple as acknowledging employees when they walk in the room. Get to know their names and whether or not they are married or have children. These are simple things, but they will show that you are putting forth the effort to get to know them.

---

## MISTAKE #55
### I Can Pick Nicknames for My Employees

You need to expend the energy to remember the names of your employees. That is the minimum necessary to getting to know them.

---

As mentioned earlier, it is also good to work on personnel issues for your employees. The schedule, holidays, and overtime are things that affect their personal and family time. This is a wonderful place to show that you care and to begin to gain their respect and trust.

### Explain What You Expect

Your team members have to know what you need from them. If you don't let them know, then how can they meet your expectations? You need to make their responsibilities clear to your people. This can include the hours they will work, lunch time, breaks, sick days, vacation, attendance, and anything else about how they will do their job.

## MISTAKE #56
### I Will Issue a Memo to Say What I Expect

You need to clearly outline your expectations to your team members. After you discuss your ideas with them, you can issue a memo as a follow up, but they need to hear it from you directly first. You should also let them ask questions.

Once you have been on the job long enough to understand what is required, you need to be clear in expressing your expectations for your employees. If anyone has suggestions, you should listen to them. That doesn't mean you have to change your mind and your requirements, but you should extend the courtesy of hearing what they have to say.

### Treat Employees Consistently

It is natural to treat some people better than others, but a manager needs to avoid this practice. All of your employees need to be treated the same. You will learn their strengths and weaknesses over time. These details will help you make more effective job assignments and to learn how to make better use of each employee, but you should not use these specifics to treat one person better or worse than another.

## MISTAKE #57
### It's So Easy to Treat Valuable Employees Better

Of course it is, but you need to treat employees the same. The more you learn about them, the easier this will be. You also need to work with and try to help employees who are more difficult. There is a possibility that you can reach them and make them more effective.

### Common Courtesy

I've learned that common courtesy isn't that common. Common courtesy doesn't denote going out of your way for others, but treating them decently with a reasonable amount of respect. This should be a normal thing for coworkers. You spend a lot of your time with your coworkers, and being courteous will save many unnecessary difficulties and hard feelings.

As the manager, it is your responsibility to set a good example for the other team members. When you notice employees being rude or thoughtless, you need to deal with that right away. Your employees will appreciate your efforts.

### Get Recognition for Your Employees

When your employees excel, their efforts should be recognized. Your job as manager puts you in a great position to give recognition within your department and to get the details to supervisors who can do more to recognize the employees. In some departments and businesses, you will have the freedom to do something special for employees who excel, such as designating them "Employee of the Month."

## MISTAKE #58
### I Don't Need to Recognize People for Just Doing Their Jobs Well

This is a time when you need to do something special for them. Employees who go above and beyond the call of duty should be recognized. This is especially true if you are commended for a job well done. Be sure to pass the recognition along to the employees, especially in front of your boss or other supervisors. Prove that you are willing to share the credit with the people who made your success possible.

Some businesses give away gift certificates or something similar to show their appreciation. In one job I had, the business owners would work a shift for one of my drivers. The employee was given the shift off and received the tips that the owners acquired. This is just one creative way to give something special to employees who go above and beyond.

### Take Responsibility

You are the manager, but that does not mean you are perfect. It also doesn't mean that you won't make mistakes. Many times, when you make a mistake, your employees know you were wrong. They'll trust you sooner if you admit your mistakes.

## MISTAKE #59
### I Made a Mistake, but No One Needs to Know

They probably already know. They will also know if you don't take the blame. You should never pass the blame on to someone else. Show your employees that they can trust you to take the blame when you make a mistake.

Some managers make a point of placing the blame with an innocent employee. This makes you look bad and will cause bad feelings within the business or department. In turn, employees will respect the fact that you accepted the blame when you were wrong.

### Recognize Employee Differences

All people are not the same. Each employee needs to be treated like an individual person. They have strengths and weaknesses that you need to deal with every day.

Recognizing differences does not mean that you should harp on employees' weaknesses. It's better to mold employees' job assignments to their abilities. Find what your employees do well and try to assign them jobs that best utilize those skills.

### Keep Your Word

Think carefully before you make promises. It's imperative that you keep promises to your employees. If you have any doubts about whether you can honor a request, then don't give your word.

## MISTAKE #60
### I Know I Promised, but It Just Isn't Possible

You made a promise and you need to keep it. If you didn't intend to follow through on your promise, then you shouldn't have given your word. Your employees need to be able to trust you, and broken promises will destroy any trust they may have.

There will be times when you cannot keep your promise because of an outside source or unavoidable situation. When this happens, talk with the employee who will be affected as soon as you find out you can't keep your promise. This quick response will help you be known as a person who does everything you can to keep your word. Your employees will appreciate the effort.

## MISTAKE #61
### I Promised My Boss and an Employee— Now What?

You need to view your word to your employee as just as important as your word to your boss. The boss depends on you and so do your employees. They all need to trust you. If your employees see that you will ignore them to keep your word to your boss, you could ruin your relationship with them.

Some managers feel a promise to their boss is more important than one to their employees. This is a dangerous attitude. Your employees depend on you, and they cannot trust you if you don't keep your promises to them. Your word to your employees is just as important as your word to your boss. They should both be able to trust you to follow through on your promises. Remember that your whole department is in trouble if there is no trust.

## LEARN FROM MISTAKES AND TAKE RESPONSIBILITY

Everyone makes mistakes from time to time. We hope they will be rare, but that depends on the people involved. Anytime you make a mistake, try to learn from it by taking a look at what went wrong and finding a way to avoid that mistake in the future.

### When Employees Make Mistakes

Learning from mistakes sounds simple, but there are times when it can be difficult. Just like you try to learn from your mistakes, you should make sure your employees learn from theirs as well. Can you implement a system in your department to evaluate errors? This wouldn't be for every little mistake, but ones that caused problems. When you evaluate mistakes, be positive. Remember, the idea is to help the employee do better the next time. Evaluating errors takes some time, but it's in the best interest of your department to find ways for everyone to learn from their mistakes.

## MISTAKE #62
### An Employee Keeps Making Mistakes. Should I Fire Him?

This is an extreme reaction. First, you should analyze what is being done wrong and try to find a way to help the employee improve. Can you sit down with him or her and try to find out why the mistake was made? Was it an intentional mistake or an accident? This makes a difference.

Some employees make mistakes because they do not listen to you. Not listening to your instructions causes many problems. When you notice this sort of behavior, you need to address the situation right away. Be clear that the employee made a mistake and try to find out why. Did the employee just ignore you? Did he think his way was better? Was he unwilling to follow directions? Each of these reasons is a problem. It would be easy to transfer the person or to fire them, but that is not the preferred solution. Try to find a way to work together successfully. You should at least try to blend your styles so you can function together effectively.

## MISTAKE #63
### Is the Employee's Mistake My Fault?

You should ask yourself if you forgot a part of the instructions. Could you have explained the situation better? Analyzing these situations can help you improve as a manager and help the employee work harder and to do a better job.

Keep in mind that evaluating mistakes will help you and the employees. It helps employees get a better grasp of how your policy works. In turn, you will get a clearer picture of your employees' attitudes and motivation.

The good news is that most employees want to do a good job. They are willing to work regular hours and give their best. Treat these employees with respect. If you don't show that you value them, their attitudes can change. If good employees get fed up, then their work and the company suffer. To save unnecessary hassles, headaches, and other problems, maintain a respectful and motivational attitude toward your employees as you swiftly and thoroughly deal with problems and mistakes.

My name is Tom Brown. I'm the owner of Copper Age (I'm also, currently, the primary artist and writer). Copper Age creates and publishes *Tales from the Copper Age,* which is the first in our line of hybrid media comics on CD. )

One of the largest mistakes that I have made so far, in my own estimation, in the process of starting this company, is the assumption that others have the same sort of ethics and values that I have.

An instance of this would be a situation that I had several months ago. I had an informal agreement with a potential associate. I assumed that since we had a verbal agreement (the conversation took place in an Instant Message session), that we would collaborate on a joint project. I thought we were equally committed. It was to be a benefit project for the people affected by Hurricane Katrina.

During our conversation, we roughed out a definition of the project and set a deadline for completion. I behaved as though we had a formal agreement. I announced this pending joint project to the press and changed my work schedule in preparation for it. The project did not happen. This set Copper Age back considerably in terms of time and momentum. It also caused embarrassment for my company because an article was published in a news and entertainment journal announcing that the project was pending and it never happened.

Tom Brown, Owner/Artist/Author Copper Age
**http://copperage-phantomegg.com**

# CHAPTER 6

# Management Skills

## CAN YOU SEE THE BIG PICTURE?

Managers need to see the big picture within their department. Many things done in the course of the day contribute to the overall well-being of your team. When employees do things, do you question them or do you see how their actions work into the overall scheme for the department?

---

### MISTAKE #64
### It's My Project; It Doesn't Involve Everyone Else

In business, few things involve only a couple of people. When you work on a project, it is interwoven with other departments, each specializing in a portion of the work.

---

This is also true when you have a large project to tackle. The large projects often require many smaller projects to be completed. Try to visualize each smaller project to see how it fits into the large project. This will make it easier for you to assign duties to your team members.

Remember that each person has to work toward the common goal. When that isn't done, any wrong steps need to be completed again and the problems need to be fixed. This can apply to special projects or day-to-day operations within your department.

## MISTAKE #65
### It's My Project; I'll Do It My Way

This mentality does not work when you are working with another department. Each manager needs to focus on his or her portion of the project, but they need to coordinate their efforts. This will lead to the overall good of each department and the business. In a company atmosphere, things need to be done for the greater good of everyone.

Do you keep up with what goes on in your department? Even though you are the manager, there are still many things going on each day that you might not be aware of. You need to keep an eye on things to keep everyone working toward the same goals.

## MISTAKE #66
### My Employees Can Handle Themselves

As the manager, you need to be in touch with your employees. Even if they are very good at their jobs, you need to be available and visible to them. This also includes following up on what they are doing and how it's going. You need to "manage" your employees.

### Stay Current on Office Communications

Take time each day to read your mail. Even if you scan it, you know if it's critical or if it can wait. If you see something new that you haven't heard about, you can ask your boss for more details. He or she should appreciate that you want to stay on top of what is happening.

---

### MISTAKE #67
#### My Interoffice Mail Doesn't Look Important

You need to take time to review your mail. There will be some that is less important, but interoffice mail is how people communicate in a large company. Don't discount anything without looking it over.

---

### Can You Train Yourself?

When you are new to a company, there is much to learn. Your boss and your employees will help with some of your education about the company, but there will probably still be things that you don't know. Can you find a way to research and learn more about the company? It would be good to ask your boss for suggestions on ways to learn more. This will help you understand the goals for the company and how you and your department fit into those plans.

---

### MISTAKE #68
#### My Boss Doesn't Spend Enough Time with Me

Your boss will do some of your training, but there will be many facets that you can learn on your own. Ask for a company manual and training aids. As you learn more, there could be other sources that you will discover. Taking the lead to learn on your own will show that you have initiative.

## Listen to Superiors

Even when you are a manager, there are people above you. If you are a manager for a small company, your only supervisor may be the owner. In a larger company, there may be several layers of management above you. Whichever situation you're in, it is critical that you listen when the people above you speak. When there is a company meeting, listen and take notes. The supervisors above you know far more about the company than you do, and it's advantageous to listen when they talk.

> ## MISTAKE #69
> ### I'm the Manager. I Shouldn't Have to Listen to Other People
>
> You're a manager, not the owner or CEO. Unless you are the owner, you will have someone else above you. Even business owners often have to listen to their board of directors and stockholders.

## Do You Have Questions?

When you have questions, ask them. It's difficult to do your job properly if you don't know what to do, how to do it, what to use, when it's due, and a dozen other details. The more time you spend wondering about what you should be doing, the less time you have to actually accomplish your job. It is very likely that your employees will have the same questions, so you need to find the answers.

## MISTAKE #70
### I Have Questions, but I Hate to Bother Anyone

When you are still learning your job, you should ask your questions. There may not always be someone handy to ask, but you can write questions down and ask later, or try to find the answer yourself. One way or another, you should get the answers to your questions.

Once you have the answers to your questions, you are in a much better position to plan and accomplish the projects and duties that were assigned to you. This will also help you understand how the smaller responsibility fits into the overall big picture.

Your employees can make better decisions if they understand how their jobs fit into the company's big picture. They don't need all the details, but general information about how their responsibilities fit into the company's plan can be very beneficial for them.

## MISTAKES #71
### I Teach My Employees That We Are the "Only Team"

While this may help your team members feel important, it erodes the idea of being part of the large company. Each team or department within the company is part of the big picture. Your employees should have pride in your department, but they also need to understand they are an integral part of the company.

Another pitfall is being too narrow minded. Being narrow-minded makes it impossible to see the big picture. If you only think about a limited amount of information, then you will miss all kinds of things that you need to make a complete and informed decision.

## MISTAKE #72
### I Figured Out the Beginning and End—
### That's Enough

To complete a project, you need a beginning, middle, and end. If you don't complete each step, then your project will be lacking. Each part of the project is important and necessary.

What would happen if you delve into the beginning of the project and rush toward the end, without considering the middle? You'll miss important steps, because the middle is an integral part of the puzzle. Likewise, you can't concentrate on the beginning and middle without thinking of the end. You have to look at all parts of the project and see them all through to the end.

How can you avoid a narrow focus? One way is to think about the full project and not just one part. Think about how the information fits together and how your job fits within the company. This is especially true when you find a problem. In order to have an effective solution, it must fit into the bigger picture. You don't need to change how you do things to see the big picture; you just need to alter how you think about things.

A last thing that might help you think about the big picture is to establish a way to share information with other departments and managers. In a large company, each department does a portion of the work, and sharing information will give you a greater understanding of how the parts fit together.

## MISTAKE #73
### I Shouldn't Have to Share All of My Plans with Others

To be truly effective, departments need to share relevant information about their projects.

### Working with Other Managers

There will be times when you will have to work with other departments and other managers. It might not be very often, but you need to cooperate when it is required. Your team members are more likely to work with other departments when they see you make the effort. Remember, they look to you for an example.

### Set Clear Goals

When you need to work with another manager, start by meeting with him or her to discuss your goals. Take notes about your meeting, including what you plan to accomplish, how you will make it happen, and who is responsible for the various duties. You can also decide ahead of time how you will evaluate the work and determine its success.

## MISTAKE #74
### I Haven't Decided What I Want to Accomplish

You need to have clear goals when you work on a project. This will give direction to your work. When you work with a manager from another department, discuss your goals together. Blending your goals for the project will benefit both of you.

### Set Milestones

In any large project it is good to have milestones, much like the various checkpoints in a race. These are places to mark your progress. Divide the project into segments and note when each segment is complete. Giving your team smaller tasks within the big project will give your team a boost throughout a long and possibly tedious project.

When working out checkpoints or milestones in a project, think of a reward for reaching each of these goals to give your team something to strive for and some recognition along the way. What about a pizza party when the first third of the project is complete? Your team will enjoy having something to look forward to and a reward for reaching that goal.

### Follow Up

When you're working on a project with another team, you need to follow up on the work being done to make sure that the project is going according to your plan. Things in life and business seldom go like we hope, so it is advisable to follow up and make sure the project is being handled and executed properly.

### MISTAKE #75
#### My Team Has It Under Control Without My Interference

Your team needs you to check on their progress. Your job as manager requires that you check on them and follow up. Remember when we talked about how their failure or success reflects on you? If you think the project is under control and it isn't, it will reflect poorly on you.

You can make sure the work is progressing and identify problems before they get out of hand. It is always good to head off a problem before it gets out of control. This is especially true in a large project. One problem in the beginning can mushroom into something much larger as the project progresses.

### Recognize Assistance

Everyone that is involved in a project should be recognized for helping, including each supervisor and all of the other teams' members. Show the people that you worked with that their efforts were noticed and appreciated. Thanking them for the specific things they contributed shows that you know they were involved and what they did.

### Lay a Foundation for Future Work Together

You should maintain a friendly relationship with the other team even after the project is complete. It is likely that you will be working with these people again and it's helpful to maintain a good working relationship. There could be opportunities to exchange employees for various projects or to work on other projects in the future. Strengthening your working relationship with other departments within a large company is beneficial for your department and the company as a whole.

## IDENTIFY THINGS YOU NEED TO IMPROVE

No matter how good we are, there are always things that we can improve. You will be more effective when you learn your limitations and how to improve your skills.

### MISTAKE #76
#### I've Learned the Job; I Don't Need to Improve

Wouldn't it be nice if that was how things worked? We can always find something to improve; we owe it to ourselves and to our employees.

You can become very frustrated in your new job—unfortunately, that is very common with new managers. Frustration does not mean you are doing anything wrong. Even if you are learning management skills and making progress with your employees, you may still be aggravated. There could be outside sources that are causing your problem, including the following:

- Your boss can make all the difference. The way your boss does his or her job will have a direct impact on you. If there are problems between you, try to keep your distance as much as possible.

- Company policies can also affect your job. The company may have policies that control how you hire, train, and treat your employees. You have to follow these policies, and that could make things more difficult for you.

- Employees can make your work life more complicated. I've found this to be particularly true when you inherit employees from a previous manager. The skill and experience level of each employee will affect how well things go for you.

- Outdated equipment and technology will make your job more difficult. You could put together a proposal asking for updated equipment, etc., for your department. Include hard facts on why the company should spend the money to upgrade. Be sure to include man-hours that are being wasted with the equipment you currently have.

### Find Out What Is Bothering You

First, figure out exactly what is bothering you. You need to narrow it down to specific problems. It is hard to tackle "everything," but if you can find a few specific things, then you can work on those one at a time.

### MISTAKE #77
#### This Job Is Driving Me Crazy

It might not be the job. Take the time to evaluate your personal situation and home life. These could contribute to your stress level. Don't jump to the conclusion that the problem is your job.

There will be times when your job isn't the problem. Has anything changed in your personal life? That could be what is causing the added stress for you. Take a close look at your life outside of work. You may find that the real problem is something at home. Has your mother-in-law come to visit? Did your spouse lose a job? Have you had a baby? These could all add more stress to your day. Make sure you know where the problems lie so you can deal with the situation better.

### Find Ways to Cope

Whenever we face problems and obstacles in life, we need to find a way to cope. In order to maintain your job and your sanity, you need a way to deal with the issues that are causing the problems. This is true whether the problem is at home or at work.

### MISTAKE #78
#### I Cannot Get Everything Done By Myself

If your stress is caused by having too much to do, your boss might be able to get you some additional help. But don't ask for help too soon—your boss needs to see you making the effort to learn and master your job.

Is there too much to do? Can you get some additional help at home? Can you talk with your boss about some help at the office? I have found that bosses are willing to find help for managers who are working hard and doing well but are overwhelmed.

If you discover there are just a couple of things that are making it difficult to cope, try to find extra time to focus on these. This will allow you to get them out of your way and to eliminate the stress they cause.

---

### MISTAKE #79
#### Everything About My Job Causing Me Stress

Sometimes it feels like everything about your job is overwhelming. It is possible it's only a couple of things in your job that are causing you difficulties. Take time to consider your responsibilities and see what's causing your hardship. You might be surprised at how easy it would be to resolve the situation and make things easier for you.

---

You may have the opposite problem. Why were you excited about the job in the first place? Are there things that need to be improved in the job? This can be an interesting way to use your time.

## GIVE YOURSELF SOME BREATHING ROOM

Here are some easy ways to see if you need more distance from your work:

- Do you wake up and think about work in the middle of the night?

- Do you frequently bring work home or go back to work after hours?

- Did you take less than two weeks of vacation in the last year?

- Are you nervous and stressed when you discipline an employee?

- Are you concerned about decisions you made?

- Do you have to be the "good guy" in the office?

- Are most of the friends you socialize with from work?

- Do you read for pleasure or is your reading work related?

Answering "yes" to one or two of these questions is not an indication of a problem, but if you do most or all of these things, give yourself a break and enjoy your time off. Make sure to take some time for yourself. Otherwise you could wake up fifteen years later and realize that all you did was work.

### Don't Feel Locked into Your Job

There is a possibility that you cannot lower your stress level. You changed your schedule, you got some help to lessen the workload, and you got some help at home, but nothing helped. What should you do if you are still unhappy? Maybe it's time to find another job. If you stay in a job that you don't like, it will only make you feel worse.

Remember that your attitude about the job will affect everyone within your department. If you are miserable, it will affect everyone else. Employees cannot be happy when their manager doesn't want to be there. Do everything possible to see if you can improve the situation, but if you can't, then it's okay to decide to leave.

# CHAPTER 7

# Improving Your Managerial Effectiveness

## HOW TO EXCEL AS A MANAGER

Taking care of your employees is one of the qualities that help you excel as a manager. There will be times when work is crazy and you don't have time to focus on proper to treatment of your employees. This could be disastrous in some situations, but the following tips will help you make decisions that keep your employees' well-being in mind.

- Be kind and sensitive toward coworkers. Your thoughts are obvious through your words and actions.

- Make other people feel special and important. One good way to do this is through positive reinforcement. When the employees do a good job, be sure to tell them.

## MISTAKE #80
### My Employees Know I Appreciate Them That's Enough

How do your employees know? Encourage your workers by commending them for doing a good job. It builds morale and doesn't cost you anything.

- When you speak with employees, watch their reactions and listen to their words. We all know people who say what you want to hear, but what do their actions and facial expressions tell you? This is especially important with employees who only say what you want. When they have a track record of saying one thing and doing another, watch their actions carefully. This can prevent additional problems in the future.

## MISTAKE # 81
### When Employees Say the Right Thing, I Rarely Look Deeper

If the employee says one thing but does another, you should watch his or her actions. Don't be a manager who listens to "yes men" but doesn't follow up to verify what they do.

- Show your employees that their desires are important to you. You show this through your decisions and the way you treat them. Keep your team members in mind and incorporate their ideas into your decisions when you can.

- Take time to appreciate the differences between people. When scheduling team members, use their strengths and weaknesses to your advantage. Some employees have certain strong points, while other employees excel in different areas.

- No matter how the actions or conversation with the employee goes, do not be defensive.

### MISTAKE #82
### One Employee Knows How to Push My Buttons

Take steps to avoid being defensive. If other employees see you get defensive, it can encourage other problems. Some employees may lose respect for you. Don't get defensive and you won't tempt others to start problems.

- Make every effort to solve personnel problems quickly. These are the most important issues for your employees, and they will appreciate your assistance.

- Be careful not to take other people for granted. A good manager needs to show appreciation for each employee.

### MISTAKE #83
### I Have A Tough Project That No One Wants to Handle. Joe Will Do Anything, So I'll Ask Him.

This is one way to take a good employee for granted. You have a difficult project and instead of spreading this kind of project around, you want someone who won't complain. That's the easy way for you, but it can cause problems with good employees. It's better to equally distribute the unappealing projects.

## ENCOURAGE POSITIVE ATTITUDES

Why should you encourage and maintain positive attitudes in your business or department?

*Positive Attitudes = Productive Employees*

*Negative Attitudes = Unproductive Employees*

We all respond better to positive attitudes. We have to spend a lot of time at our jobs, and the majority of us prefer to work in a positive environment with positive people.

## MISTAKE #84
### *Mary Has a Bad Attitude, But She Has Seniority, So She Should Be in Charge of the Project*

Mary may have seniority in the department, but you would be rewarding her for a bad attitude. Wouldn't it be better for department morale to assign someone who works hard and has a good attitude? It could show Mary that good attitudes are appreciated and needed to excel in your department.

### Attitudes You Should Avoid

A company should include a group of people working toward a common goal. We've talked about this before. It's important to work as a group toward the "big picture." Your comments and actions make a difference in how you are treated in your department. Keep in mind that certain attitudes are better suited for specific companies; attitudes that are satisfactory in one business may not be acceptable in another.

The majority of us are politically correct in our behavior and attitudes. You can have independent thoughts, but avoid radical and extreme comments at work. Those comments make you stand out and can cause you problems.

## MISTAKE #85
### My Team Is the Best

That comment shows pride in your team. However, what attitude do you display? Do you belittle the other people within the company? Healthy competition is good, but you should avoid going too far. Feel good about your team's successes, but not at the expense of someone else.

A few tips for your behavior would include the following:

- Let your team know that you will do your share of the work.

## MISTAKE #86
### I'll Do My Share, But None of the "Dirty" Jobs

Everyone in the department should take turns doing the less desirable jobs. Show your team members that you will work by their side. They will respect you for this.

- If you have the attitude that you will win and your employees will lose, you won't be around for long. You won't earn respect, and you may create additional problems.

## MISTAKE #87
### I Will Fight for Everything My Department Needs

You can take this stand and fight the system, but it won't help you in the long run. Everyone needs to give sometimes. You don't want the reputation of being a bully.

- Every productive and long-lasting company goes through changes at times. Fighting the changes will make things more difficult for everyone.

> ### *MISTAKE #88*
> #### *My Department Doesn't Need to Change*
> You may have no choice. A positive and flexible attitude makes things go smoother for you and the department. Your boss and other supervisors will appreciate your attitude.

- Share the credit when others help you accomplish a goal. It doesn't hurt if you give them some extra credit. This makes them feel good about their jobs and themselves. They will also feel good about you as their manager.

## Qualities of a Mensch

I recently learned the word "mensch," and I wanted to share the positive and effective traits with you. The definition of a mensch is a person with admirable characteristics, such as fortitude and firmness of purpose.

Isn't that a wonderful description of a manager? There are some wonderful traits that are attributed to a mensch that each manager can put into practice.

- Always continue to learn. You are never too old to learn something new. Learning keeps your mind and soul young.

## MISTAKE #89
### You Can't Teach an Old Dog New Tricks

We have all heard this comment, and many of us have probably used it, but it's not true. No matter what your age or experience, there is always more to learn, in business and in life.

- Be responsible and kind to yourself and others. Positive or negative behavior can be contagious. Which behavior do you want to deal with each day?

## MISTAKE #90
### I Have a Question; I'll Interrupt My Boss's Meeting to Get an Answer Right Now

It's good to ask your boss questions. However, it's not good to interrupt a meeting. Can you work on something else and wait until your boss is available? It gives your employees a good example and shows respect for your boss.

- Ask questions frequently in order to learn more. These questions should be asked in an appropriate way, so consider when and where you ask them.

- Pay attention to verbal and nonverbal communication when you speak with others. This is especially important with your coworkers. Do your words convey one meaning while your actions show another?

- Promptly respond to all messages you receive. This is true whether they are e-mail, voice mail or "snail" mail. If you don't know the answer, tell the sender that you will find it and get back to them.

## MISTAKE #91
### That Message Was Sent "Snail" Mail, So I'll Take My Time Answering It

The type of message your received doesn't make a difference in how quickly you should reply. Some people prefer different types of communication. That doesn't mean they should have to wait longer for your response. Answer all messages as quickly as possible.

- Respect the feelings of others. That is important in every aspect of your life. It's the Golden Rule: Treat others like you want to be treated.

- When you talk or deal with others, be honest, sensitive, and direct. Each of these qualities helps people to trust, respect, and believe you.

## MISTAKE #92
### I Don't Want to Answer That Question, So I Will Be Evasive

Most people know when you are avoiding them or their questions. One way to earn respect and trust is to be honest and upfront. Answer directly, even if it's a tough question; this is especially true for hard questions.

- When you act or speak, don't leave room for confusion. Address the subject that is being dealt with at the time; don't talk around it.

- Don't be defensive. There may be situations where someone tries to put you on the spot, but remain calm.

- A cooperative and helpful attitude should dictate your actions; work will go smoother for you and your employees.

- Ask for your employees' thoughts and opinions. This helps them see that you respect their ideas and will benefit you in many ways.

### MISTAKE #93
### I Want to Do It My Way, But I'm Not Sure What to Do

If you have questions that your boss hasn't cleared up, ask your team members for their input. They can give you valuable information, and they'll respect you for asking.

- When you are in a jam, ask for help. Let your team members know you need them. They will respond better if this happens only occasionally instead of all the time.

- Give plenty of praise to your team when they deserve it. Be sincere when you offer praise and recognition. If you sound insincere, they will know.

The phrase "Build a bridge to healthy communication," which I found in an article, is a nice summary of how to communicate with your employees. That phrase conjured up positive thoughts for me and summarizes the qualities of a mensch. As a manager, how can you build a bridge to healthy communication with your employees?

Employees may forget many things about a conversation or a duty that you assign to them, but they will remember when you make them feel good or bad—especially when you make them feel bad. We have all had unpleasant bosses, and we don't remember them fondly. How often have you complained about these bosses to your friends?

## MISTAKE #94
### I Can Be a Tyrant Too

Did you ever have a boss who was a tyrant? If you have, you probably didn't like working with him or her. Your team members don't want to work for a tyrant either. When you see other bosses mistreating their employees, that doesn't mean you should do the same. Take the initiative to set yourself apart by being respectful to your team.

When you worked for a tyrant, did you promise that you would be different? Many people make this promise to themselves. This is especially true when cruel actions and scathing words are fresh in your mind. For the benefit of your team, keep that promise you made.

You will learn that it isn't easy to manage people. The more people you manage, the tougher it becomes. Do you have employees who make your job difficult? Be aware that all managers have employees who cause problems at times. As you implement the tips, techniques, and suggestions in this book, you will have fewer problem employees.

## MISTAKE #95
### One Employee Gets on My Nerves, and I Know How to Spite Him

Resist the temptation to do spiteful things to employees who get under your skin. There are times when we think about this kind of thing, but do not act on it.

When I managed a pizza restaurant; I had to learn a great deal in a short time. There were several stores in our franchise, each with distinct characteristics. I had worked in them all, but the store that I managed had very distinct situations that we had to deal with. It was secluded and we were open after most other businesses had closed, so safety was an issue. The town we delivered in had train tracks in many locations, which delayed our deliveries. This was before cell phones were reasonably priced, so I couldn't call drivers when they were gone for long periods.

## MISTAKE #96
### I'm New to this Business, So My Team Will Suffer While I Learn

You need to learn the job in a timely manner. Your team members shouldn't suffer because you are new. It is good to ask your boss and employees who have been with the company for a long time for advice. If something seems unusual, ask questions of a dependable and trustworthy source.

I had recently moved to the town and worked long hours. It was a struggle to get to work, clean my uniforms, and get the store and crew ready for the return of the college students. I didn't have time to ride around town to learn where everything was. On a busy Friday night, I got a crash course on the layout of the town. Soon, I learned my way around and things went smoother.

What's my point? Even though I had worked in similar situations, there were things about this new situation that I had to learn and take into account when I dealt with the employees. I didn't let my team suffer while I was still learning the ropes.

## MISTAKE #97
### I Worked in Another Department So I Know Enough

Even if the department was similar, you will still have things to learn. I've found it better to go into a new job assuming I have things to learn, and I'm never disappointed. Even if you understand the job, you need to become familiar with your new employees and how the department fits into the "big picture" of the company.

When you start working in a new department at the same company or in a similar position to one you've held before, remember that it's still a new job. Talk with your employees and ask them what difficulties they are dealing with each day. Figure out who the best workers are and ask for their input about how the department could run smoother. Some ideas might not be useful, but you might be amazed at the ideas you will get. These people do the job every day and are in the best position to give ideas to improve the overall work environment.

## MISTAKE #98
### If My Employees Knew How to Handle the Department, They Would Be in Charge

That's not necessarily true. Some people may not be qualified to manage or may not want to be in charge, but this does not decrease the value of their experience or knowledge they bring to the job.

It's also important to think before you act. It seems simple, but how many people really do it? Thinking before you act can save you a lot of hassle and unnecessary problems. Sometimes this can be difficult, especially when you have ten things to do at once. Every manager has been in this situation. You have several deadlines looming, there's a 2-foot pile of mail, five employees have questions, and your boss is on the phone. It's hard find time to make a solid decision when you're surrounded by things that need to be done. Decision making under fire does become easier. It's amazing how many of these things you can do effectively at once with practice.

There are times when you need to make an announcement or schedule the agenda for a staff meeting. When you do these things, take a few minutes to consider your employees' reactions. If you think a specific person will react badly, it might be good to first discuss the information with that person privately.

### MISTAKE #99
#### The Announcement Needs to be Made, No Matter What People Think About It

Even when an announcement is needed, consider how your team members will react. It's best to handle major announcements or changes with tact. Be prepared for harsh reactions.

When I knew that some people would be unhappy about an announcement, I sometimes assigned them to work outside the department during the meeting. Then I went to the area where they were working to talk with them so I could tell them the details before they returned to the department. They were sometimes upset with me at first, but because they cared about the well-being of the department, they understood.

## MISTAKE #100
### It's Probably Better to Tell Everyone About Changes at Once and Handle the Fallout

That creates a difficult meeting and conflict. If some people will have problems with decisions or changes, it is better to deal with them individually. Most of your team members will handle announcements fine, but be prepared for people who will be upset. When you talk to them separately, you prevent bigger problems and conflict.

Do you think about your employees' needs when you plan a project? Getting to know them will make this easier. You can ask for their thoughts in meetings and when you talk or work with them. Find time to work side by side with your employees, when there aren't deadlines or a crisis situation. Working together will help you get to know each other better.

## MISTAKE #101
### I Don't Have Time to Work With My Employees

This doesn't need to be 40 hours a week, but you need to find time to work together. Working side by side gives you a chance to learn more about them. This is important to effectively utilize your team members.

When your employees walk by your desk, do you call out for them to do something for you? It might seem innocent, but is that the only time you speak to them? Do you ask them to do something each time they walk past? Many employees will be happy to help, but some will wonder why you can't get your own coffee or office supplies. Don't make your employees think that you are too good for certain activities around the office.

## MISTAKE #102
### He Was Walking Toward the Coffee Machine Anyway

This may seem silly to you, but some employees remember every time you ask them to do something for you. I've known managers who sat behind a desk with their feet up and expected their employees to do everything for them. I never knew any of these managers to be respected by their teams.

Before you became a manager, you had time to think of everything you'd do if you were the boss. Remember how past bosses have treated you. What did they do that made you feel bad? Avoid these things completely. Keep that promise you made long ago to never be a bad manager. On the other hand, what did former managers do or say to make you feel good about yourself and your job? Try to remember some specifics and use them when you interact with your team members.

After a buy-out of a mature business, the new owners installed a new general manager and one other key manager but left the long-time operations manager in place. This person had been in the job over 20 years and had rigid notions of what got done and how it was done.

As the new owners reactivated idle equipment and introduced new product lines, the old line manager was a constant block. He blocked new ideas openly and if not successful, worked to block them in stealth. When the new owners sent his subordinates off for training in new management techniques, he would spend days when they returned "brainwashing" the new ideas out of them.

Even after he was forced into early retirement, this old line manager would go out to lunch weekly with a group of his former subordinates trying to continue to influence them. Only when the subordinates were forbidden to go to lunch with him did his influence begin to wane.

Hill Kemp, Author
**www.capitoloffense.com**

# CHAPTER 8

# Dealing with People Outside Your Department

## WORKING WITH OTHER GROUPS

This chapter applies to managers who work in a company with multiple departments. If you are a manager in a small company or if you manage a small business, this information might not apply to you.

### When Other Work Groups Take Your Projects

It's frustrating when other groups or departments are called on to handle projects that your team should be working on, but there are times when there's nothing you can do. What if your boss calls you in to tell you he's giving some of your responsibilities to another manager? There can be various reasons for this action. Your boss may be satisfied with your work and may believe you need a break. Or he may not be happy with the work your team is doing. In that case, he would reassign the project to another group. Find out why he made the decision. If you feel the decision was inappropriate, you can talk to your boss in a rational manner and discuss your concerns.

## MISTAKE #103
### My Boss Is Worried Because I've Been Working So Hard

This probably isn't why your boss reassigned the project. The most likely answer would be that he isn't happy with the work your group is turning out. He may be concerned about your turnaround time to complete projects, and he feels it's necessary to reassign the work.

When your boss is concerned and trying to lighten our workload, it isn't usually a compliment. It's a situation where you need to regain control. Did you complain to your boss or others about your workload? Your boss might feel you cannot handle your work assignments and that it's better to reassign projects to another group. You need to know if your boss feels that your group isn't qualified to handle the work that was assigned, and then do everything possible to fix the situation.

## MISTAKE #104
### I Should Notify My Boss That My Group Has Too Much Work

This isn't a good idea. Find ways to redistribute or streamline the work. If your boss feels your group cannot handle the workload, that reflects poorly on you. He or she may decide to give your work to others. You don't want to start this chain of events.

When your boss starts taking work away from your group, it will take time to recover. Have a meeting and let your group know that it isn't something to celebrate. As a group, you must figure out what went wrong and find ways to fix it. You must change the way your boss sees your group.

---

### MISTAKE #105
### My Group Can Enjoy a Little Break for a Couple of Weeks and Then I'll Talk to My Boss

Now is the time to be concerned. Your boss shouldn't see you taking it easy. In a large company, it's easy to be replaced and phased out. Make it clear that your team wants more work, not less.

---

There could be several reasons why the work was taken from your group:

- Your boss, a customer, or another supervisor might be unhappy with your work. Turnaround time could be the issue. It might be the number of people that were needed or the quality of the work that was done. Find out what the problem was and tell your boss you're determined to improve in the deficient areas.

---

### MISTAKE #106
### If Only One Customer Is Unhappy, What's the Big Deal?

It only takes one unhappy customer to cause problems for you. You always need to work hard to please your customers; their satisfaction is an indicator of how well you did your job.

---

- Is there another group in the company that is taking on extra work to look better? Your team needs to do the same thing. Bosses like initiative. When the boss starts taking work away from you, it's time to shift gears and work harder. Tell your boss that your group wants to find ways to prove themselves, and then do a great job on the next project.

## MISTAKE #107
### If Another Team Wants the Work, They Should Get to Do It

Are there particular projects that you do well? Volunteer for these sorts of jobs. This shows initiative and a willingness to get more work. Bosses appreciate these traits.

When you get a challenging project, be sure to do it well. If your team struggles with the project, take the initiative to ask questions and get the help you need to succeed. It's good to find ways to challenge your team. Keep in mind that it takes different things to challenge different people. Over time, you will learn what sort of things challenge your employees.

## MISTAKE #108
### We Volunteered to Do the Project; That's Enough

When your team is assigned a project, you need to do a superior job. It's important to show the initiative to get the job, but it's even more important to show the motivation to complete the job well.

### Focus on Satisfying the Customer

In business, you have to focus on the customer. If there are no customers, we aren't needed. That's why managers must focus on keeping customers happy. In many businesses, the manager has direct communication with the customers. In other businesses, the customer deals with a series of people who convey their needs directly to the manager working on their project. However your company is established, you must ensure there is a line of communication so the customer is happy with your work.

> ## MISTAKE #109
> ### There Are Too Many People Between the Customer and Me
>
> Find ways to get the specific information on what your customers need. Ask your boss whom you should speak with to find out what the customer wants. Can you meet with the customer or talk on the phone? If you get a chance to meet or talk, behave in a professional manner. This shows the customer that you took time to get your ideas together and shows respect for them and their time.

Did your boss hear the customer wasn't happy with your work? Being told the work didn't meet their expectations isn't enough. You need details about what wasn't satisfactory so that you can fix the things that weren't up to par. Your boss should appreciate that you want to improve your work quality in order to make the customer happy.

Some things you need to know in order to make your customers happy include the following:

- What do they need?

- How do they intend to use it?

- When do they need it?

- Who will use the product?

- What additional things would they like to incorporate in the product?

These basic things will give you an idea of how to make the product more useful to the customer. Gather this information, and then set a realistic time frame for when you expect to complete the customer's project. Timelines are critical, but be realistic. If your time frame isn't acceptable, evaluate your plan and make adjustments. When a timeline looks impossible, discuss it with your boss and the customer to find a reasonable way to accomplish the task.

There are usually questions in the course of a project. Find out who your contact is before problems arise, and notify that person immediately when you have questions. Discussing these concerns with your boss shows that you are concerned with making the customer happy.

### Pay Attention to the Needs of the Company

Are there any other reasons for your boss to take the project away from your team? Did you ask for too much help from other departments? Is the company reorganizing in an effort to scale back?

## MISTAKE # 110
### I Don't Need to Worry About the Whole Company

You should be concerned about how you and your team fit into the company's plan. If you are a manager who only thinks about your team, your boss and other supervisors will notice that. It's important to be a team player and to be concerned with how your team fits into the company.

Many companies reevaluate their organization from time to time. Periodically, I would review the workload and employees to find ways to save money by cutting man-hours. This required the remaining employees to work harder, but it also allowed me to create the best crew while saving the company money.

### Do Not Accept "Dead End" Projects

New managers can be the scapegoats for all sorts of situations. Other managers might try to dump their unwanted projects on you. Review a project thoroughly before you accept it from anyone. It is possible that a more experienced manager is trying to pawn off an undesirable, complicated, or boring project.

If your team accepts a difficult project from another manager, then you're taking a chance on making your team look bad just to please another manager. But don't let your boss think that your group can't handle complicated projects. If you do, you'll need to prove yourself all over again.

## MISTAKE #111
### Another Manager Dumped a Project on Me

A good rule of thumb is to review the project carefully before you accept or refuse it. There could be times when another manager wants to give you a boring or difficult project. But it might be a project that could make your team look good. This is why it's good to study the details before you make a final decision whether or not to accept the project.

### Reorganize Your Team

If you're having trouble working with other work groups, then reorganizing your team might help you work better within the context of the company. An effective manager knows the members of his or her team and finds the best way to utilize their abilities. Some people may be better at analyzing and others at organizing. One may be great at design and another can research anything. Each of these skills is necessary, and you should assign their tasks based on these abilities.

## MISTAKE #112
### Jenny Is Good at Design, but I Need Her to Do Research for This Job

You can try that approach, but be ready to give Jenny a hand. Some people cannot research effectively. You can assign tasks that the employees don't excel in, but be ready to give the help they need to succeed on those tasks.

When you are given a boring or repetitive project, can you make it easier? Some teams have done projects the same way for years. There could be a great new way to reorganize your employees to make the project better. Discovering these alternatives will impress your boss and demonstrate the creativity and ability that your team possesses.

### Ensure Your Group Will Excel

Once your boss begins to take work away from your group, it is more critical that your group excel with any project it undertakes. Your team has something to prove and they need to prove it. Have a meeting with your boss and discuss the team's strong points. Are there weak points that he or she could give you advice about? This depends on your boss and whether you can discuss these problems.

## MISTAKE #113
### It Should Be Enough That We Offered to Do More

It might seem that way, but it's not true. Offering to do more work is the first step. You need to prove you can actually do the job. Strive to excel at the project and impress your boss with the qualifications within your team.

When you undertake a new project, take the chance to tell your boss about the things your team excels at and how it pertains to the current job. Your team may have found a better, quicker, or cheaper way to do the job. If so, share that with your boss. It could help other departments within the company.

## MISTAKE #114
### We Figured Out a Better Way to Do the Job, but We Want to Keep It to Ourselves

Share the discovery with your boss and the other managers. If the project is done within the department on a regular basis, share the new ideas with coworkers; it makes your team look good and helps the company.

Be careful when you find better ways to do boring and repetitive jobs. This could mean that your team will get all of those jobs. If you don't want all those projects, you can train other people so they would also be qualified to do that type of project. This demonstrates you will help other groups within the company.

### Don't Let Other Managers Push You Around

Managers must accept feedback and criticism from their bosses and supervisors. However, they do not have to accept criticism from other managers. During the early days of your job as a manager, other managers may tell you how to do your job. You must decipher whether the manager is being helpful or trying to cause a problem. Are you being tormented or only teased? Do other managers within the company want to take advantage of the new manager? Evaluate the situation to determine if that is the case. Can you handle it yourself or do you need to involve your boss?

## MISTAKE #115
### If Another Manager Criticizes Me, I Will Lash Out at Him or Her

Watch how the manager behaves with other people. Are you being singled out? Lashing out isn't the first thing you should do. You could make the problem worse if you overreact.

Sometimes it's best to ignore the person who criticizes you. Many people will stop bothering you if they discover you won't get mad or react to them. But some people will treat you worse if they believe you won't react. Ignore it at first and then decide it you need to take further action.

## MISTAKE #116
### I'll Let My Boss Handle It

It isn't usually a good idea to involve your boss in the beginning. Give it time and watch how the person treats other people. If you're the only one being criticized, then something may need to be done about the situation.

Before you bring your boss into the situation, try to work things out with the other supervisor. It's better to handle a situation yourself instead of bringing your boss into every little squabble. When you speak with the other person, make him or her understand that you are also a manager and their behavior is unacceptable. Make it clear, in a polite and rational manner, that you are there to stay and won't be pushed around. If you notice the criticism takes on a harsher tone, then discuss the situation with your boss. Your supervisor should know what action to take based on past situations.

## MISTAKE #117
### I'm Tired of the Criticism So I Will Talk to My Boss

If you are being singled out, you may not be able to fix the problem. In that case, your boss needs to take action. You should document what happened; this will help your boss deal with it more effectively.

Try to find a way to resolve the situation without making it escalate to another level. Chances are that you will continue to work together, so resolve difficult situations in the easiest and least confrontational way possible. You can try to fix the situation, but if that doesn't work, then discuss the details with your boss.

### Dealing with Office Politics

How can you get the resources you need within the company? This can include supplies or additional manpower for a special project. Long-term managers have learned the tricks to getting results in their department and the company. You need to find ways to get what you need for your team.

Try to get what you want and need without being a nuisance to anyone, especially to your boss. Some projects require more interaction with other departments. These people may hesitate to help you, but motivate them to work with you. It is important that you don't pressure them. Many busy people will "accidentally" lose your request if you pressure them.

Your approach should be adjusted depending on who you are dealing with. Most people respond to kind words and a patient attitude. A harsh and demanding demeanor doesn't work. The person may be more helpful because you are new to your job.

Most managers remember how hard it was when they got started and they might make the effort to help you. Show them that you appreciate their help.

## MISTAKE #118
### I'll Say That I Need It Now and I Don't Want Any Excuses

While I understand your frustration, this is not the best approach. If you begin making demands, it's likely your request will be moved to the bottom of the pile. There are some legitimate excuses, and with practice, you will learn which excuses are realistic and which were invented.

You might run into someone who wants to discourage new managers from asking for assistance. This could be that person's way of getting people to bother them less. Don't let this stop you.

Is someone in another department working on something for you? If so, talk with them directly and give them a gentle push. You could reiterate that you need the item and mention your time frame. It is usually more effective for you to ask yourself.

## MISTAKE #119
### I'll Go Around Juan to Get a Quicker Answer

Be careful about "going around" department managers. Do you like it when they go around you to talk with your team members? You probably don't, so extend the same courtesy to them.

I learned that some people have trouble meeting deadlines, and it's better to move the timeline a few days. This saves you the last-minute frenzy of trying to get the work done on time. Simply say you need their work by a certain date, whether that is the project deadline or not. When you word it that way, you are telling them the truth and it will eliminate problems at the last minute.

Can you request help from people in various departments? This will take the stress off of one department, and there are usually several people in a company who are qualified to help on a project. It is human nature to go to the most willing and agreeable people first. However, this can cause problems when you call on the same people every time. Try to find new people when you have a project that doesn't have a tight deadline. This gives you time to work with new people and see if others have the abilities you need.

## MISTAKE #120
### Mike Is Great to Work with, and I Don't Want to Waste Time Finding Someone Else

It is wonderful that Mike can help, but it's good to find other people to work with you. What if you have a deadline and Mike isn't available? There will be times when your favorite people are busy with another project and you will need to find someone else.

Can you adjust what you need from your employees? There are times when one person can't do everything you need and you will need to be flexible. This can include people you work with and the tasks you need them to do. The sooner you begin a project, the more time and flexibility you will have. Enjoy the flexibility when it's possible because there will be instances when you have no choice and cannot make adjustments.

## MISTAKE #121
### This Project Isn't a Rush; We Can Take Our Time

There will be plenty of rush projects. When you have a project with a more flexible time frame, use the time to fine-tune your approach. Don't waste time; you should use the additional time constructively by searching for new people and methods to make the same project run smoothly when it is a rush.

When you have a project that isn't a rush, use your time wisely, but don't pressure the people who are involved. There will be projects when you have to make people rush their part of the work or push the project to completion, but don't rush when you don't need to.

### Use Creativity to Acquire Needed Resources

New managers can usually get the supplies and resources they need. People will work with you and help in the beginning. Don't take this for granted, and remember to show the proper appreciation for the cooperation you receive. This can help you build good and lasting relationships with others within the company.

## MISTAKE #122
### While People Are Helping Me, Maybe I Should Take Advantage of Their Generosity

Don't use people when they try to help you. To build strong working relationships with others, don't take advantage of their kindness. Take only what you need and thank them for their help. This will go a long way in building a good relationship with them.

While you are getting settled into the department, take time to see what supplies or equipment you may need. Don't worry about whether you have enough employees, because at that stage, you won't know. Your employees can give you information about the equipment and supplies you have and if there are any problems.

## MISTAKE #123
### It Doesn't Look Like I Have Enough Employees

When you are new to the department, you don't know if there are enough employees. Take your time and see what sort of tasks you receive and learn to utilize the people you have. You may need more people in the future, but that isn't your first priority.

Show your boss you have taken an inventory of your department and you're taking initiative to make things better for your team. Make a concise list of the things you need the most and why you need them. This shows that you gave your list thought and can help convince your boss they're legitimate needs. If you ask for more than you really need, your boss might ignore your request.

## MISTAKE #124
### My Boss Should Make Sure We Get Everything on My List

That would be nice, but it probably won't happen. Your boss is limited in how much he or she can give each department. Most supervisors have to submit an annual budget, and they are expected to stay within those limits. Your boss should do what is possible, but don't be unrealistic in your expectations.

No matter how hard you work on your list, keep in mind that you probably won't get everything. There is also a chance your boss won't give you anything. If that happens, save your list and submit another request in the future. If there are certain times during the year when you can submit requests for big purchases, it could simply be the wrong time to request money or supplies.

### Getting Around Problems and Delays

In a large company, many things will be beyond your control. This is something you need to accept. With numerous departments, employees, and supervisors involved, you can't snap your fingers and make things happen. A manager in a small business has a better chance of making things happen.

Sometimes your employees can cause problems. Some employees might have been born to procrastinate. Indecisiveness is another trait that causes unnecessary delays. There are also people who cause problems and hassles to feel more powerful. Is there a power struggle? If someone wants to usurp your authority, then he or she could cause problems for you.

## MISTAKE #125
### I Can't Tell Which Employees Are Causing Problems

Watch carefully to see who is really accomplishing anything. Some people push papers around on their desk but don't complete things. Others spend a good part of their time finding ways to cause problems. Keep an eye on productivity and activity. These will help you see where the problems lie.

Is there someone in your department who doesn't want the project to be done? This person can find ways to stop or hold up the job. Keep your eyes open for people who are opposed to the project or seem busy but aren't really working.

Each of these behaviors can and will cause delays and holdups on your project. You need to learn to identify these problems and find ways to get past them. Any obstacle can be overcome, and the sooner you discover the problem, the easier it will be to get past it. When you discover problems, try the following to resolve them:

- Push the procrastinator to get busy.

- Try not to involve procrastinators unless it is necessary.

- Find a dependable person to do the job.

- Get the procrastinator to sign a statement with a deadline commitment.

- Is there a way to avoid the problem?

- Will the procrastinator respond better to someone else?

- If all else fails, get your boss involved.

When you first become a manager, you may not understand how the office politics work. Learn to work these situations for the good of your department. If you don't learn how to do this, it could affect your ability to get your job done.

You are the new person and don't know which people are friends and allies. This means that you shouldn't publicly criticize anyone within the company. If someone tries to drag you into a negative conversation, avoid the situation and keep your thoughts to yourself. You should also watch how your employees and coworkers deal with one another on the job.

Your relations with other employees and managers will directly affect how things go for you in your department. It is critical that you learn to work with others in order to successfully and effectively do your job. Don't expect to learn everything in the very beginning, but you will learn how to work with others within the company as you become more experienced.

One of the biggest problems that the accounts payable department has is dealing with rush checks. In fact, 60 percent of the readers of *Accounts Payable Now & Tomorrow*, a newsletter for professionals interested in payment issues, identified rush checks as their biggest check problem. These are "emergency" check requests that require someone in the department to stop what they are doing and draw a manual check to meet an obligation that typically should have been paid earlier. While in an ideal world companies would simply refuse to issue checks in this manner, this just doesn't work in the real world.

## *Worst-Case Scenario*

Here's an unfortunately all-too-common occurrence. A purchasing professional neglects to approve an invoice for payment for several weeks. This is not done out of malice; it's simply not that important to the purchasing associate. Then, when a new order is placed, the supplier refuses to ship until the outstanding invoice is paid. At this point, the purchasing professional makes a mad search of his desk and finds the invoice, scribbles an okay to pay, and rushes to accounts payable demanding a check immediately.

Now, if this were a rare occurrence, accounts payable would probably comply. But at many companies, it's the same individuals over and over. This is a huge problem that disrupts the work cycle in accounts payable. Plus, these checks are the leading cause of duplicate payments and fraud. Here's where the trouble starts: If the accounts payable manager digs in her heels and refuses to issue the check, the purchasing associate often goes to the accounts payable manager's boss, typically the controller. If the manager's decision is overridden, as it often is, the accounts payable manager's position is weakened in future encounters, the bad behavior is rewarded, and an endless repeat cycle of inefficient processes occurs. Is there a better way?

## *Solutions*

Whether dealing with unreasonable purchasing executives or employees in other departments, there are a number of ways that managers can handle

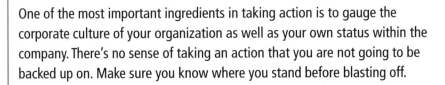

difficult interactions with other work groups. For starters, do what you can to avoid head-on collisions where there is a definite winner and a definite loser. Although you may occasionally win a battle, it will be a short-lived victory.

Whenever you deal with another group, let them know what your requirements and deadlines are. In this example, make purchasing aware of the deadlines and check run schedule. Reminder notices are not a bad idea, either. These can be sent relatively easily via e-mail and are especially effective when approaching year-end or monthly closes.

One of the most important ingredients in taking action is to gauge the corporate culture of your organization as well as your own status within the company. There's no sense of taking an action that you are not going to be backed up on. Make sure you know where you stand before blasting off.

If someone is requesting an action that is out of the normal cycle, make it difficult for them. In the rush-check example, require a senior sign-off on the request. You will be surprised to find how many people decide they really don't need that rush check if it means they have to explain to a senior vice president why they are in this predicament.

Finally, if you find yourself in the position of having to do something for another group that you really don't think you should, make the most of it. Do it pleasantly and keep notes. If there is something you want from that other group, this is the perfect opportunity to ask for it. Of course, they are not likely to comply if you are only issuing the check because the controller insisted that you do it. This is where knowing the political climate comes in handy.

Working with other groups can be a challenge. But the savvy professional who understands the ramifications of doing things well will make the most of those interactions.

Mary S. Schaeffer, Editorial Director
*Accounts Payable Now & Tomorrow*, **www.ap-now.com**

# CHAPTER 9

# Support Your Boss

Your boss has the ability to make your job easier or more difficult, so your working relationship with him or her is very important. Team members need to understand that you answer to your boss. We'll discuss ways you can show support for your boss, as well as times when it's not wise to support him. We'll cover how to protect yourself while you do your job.

## SHOW SUPPORT FOR YOUR BOSS

Have there been times when you thought you had done an excellent job but your boss didn't agree? Could it be that your boss had a different idea about how to handle the project? That could be at the root of your boss's displeasure.

Take a look at the project and see if there is anything that your boss could complain about. I knew a manager who worked with a customer who planned to spend a couple of million dollars to replace existing equipment. During the course of the project, the manager realized the equipment could be refurbished, saving the customer a lot of money. When the manager returned to his office, he discovered his boss was unhappy with the results. Understandably, the manager was confused.

Why do you think the boss was upset? The boss's stance was that the customer is always right, and you don't question their decisions. He wanted the team to work on the project using the customer's criteria. A suggestion to refurbish their equipment wasn't what the customer wanted.

How could you avoid this problem? If you have a sweeping suggestion for your customer, discuss it with your boss. This allows you to get your boss's feedback about your plan. Explain the plan and your reasoning. You and your boss can form a joint decision before you approach the customer.

## MISTAKE #126
### I Don't Understand Why the Boss Is Unhappy; I Saved the Customer Money

There are many people, especially business owners, who don't like to be told they are wrong. When the customer has definite ideas, think carefully about making suggestions.

How can you get and stay in your boss's good graces? Here are some tips to help you and your team:

- Listen to what you boss says and watch how he or she handles various situations. You can learn a lot from a person's actions.

- What actions does your boss reward and what does he or she not reward? These details can give you insight into your boss's thoughts and motivations. Look beyond the surface to learn why the rewards were given or withheld. If you cannot find the correlation, ask your boss. He or she should appreciate your initiative and interest.

- Ask your boss for feedback. Find out what your boss thinks and what motivates him or her. How can you adjust to your boss's style?

Keep in mind that effective bosses thoroughly explain their desires and hopes for the team. You want these actions from your boss. Your employees want and need the same things from you.

> ## MISTAKE #127
> ### I Shouldn't Have to Explain My Thoughts to My Employees
>
> You expect your boss to explain his desires and actions. Your team members expect the same from you. They need to understand you and your goals in order to work effectively.

### Work with Your Boss

Your responsibilities as a manager are to keep your department running smoothly and to make your boss look good. Does that sound unreasonable to you? Isn't that what you expect from your team members? You want them to do a good job and to make you look good, and your boss wants the same from you.

You need to run your department and projects smoothly. In the process, you are responsible for listening to your boss's direction and keeping him or her happy. This moves you toward the goal of making your boss successful. Some things can make this easier:

- When you realize there may be complaints from your customers, your boss needs to be notified. There may be ways your boss can head off a problem or prepare for complaints.

- It's good to show your boss the quality of your work. Your boss is the person who needs to appreciate the effort you put into your work and who can show appreciation for your efforts.

### Inform Your Boss About Your Success

Do you have a suggestion for a change that will improve conditions or save money? What should you do when your boss insists that you shouldn't implement your suggestions? First, explain the reasons for these changes and the benefits to the company. If the change has already been implemented, explain the benefits that have been experienced.

---

## MISTAKE #128
### My Ideas Are Solid; I Shouldn't Have to Go Through My Boss

People are resistant to change. When you talk with your boss and have his or her support, that paves the way for your suggestions. This also helps your boss keep an eye on your success and progress. At evaluation time, you will be glad your boss is well informed about your work.

---

Do you feel that you know everything? Whatever your answer is, I can assure you that you don't. The same is true about your boss. Being in charge doesn't make a person perfect. There will be times when you must tactfully explain your reasoning and justify your suggestions. Gauge your boss's reactions when you voice your opinions.

When your boss questions you, there are some simple steps you should follow. First, make a complete list of the reasons and benefits. Make notes about the details to share with your boss. Second, be confident and tactful when you talk with your boss. If you believe in your idea, make that clear. Finally, listen to your boss's feedback and be prepared to make necessary adjustments. Once you explain your reasoning, your boss may have suggestions to make it work better.

## MISTAKE #129
### My Boss Wants the Project Details; I'll Just Rattle Them Off to Him

It's better to make notes before talking with your boss. He might ask questions and interrupt your thoughts. A written summary for him is a nice touch. That gives him a place to make notes, and he can file it in your personnel file. When it's time for your evaluation, it will remind him of your thorough and complete work.

### Represent Your Boss

You must be loyal to your boss. You are a representative for him or her within the company. Managers who don't represent their bosses will lose their confidence.

Employees may belittle your boss and encourage you to join in. Don't fall into this trap, but know that employees might resent your disloyalty to them. As the manager, you work between your boss and your employees. During this process, maintain your loyalty to both factions. It's your responsibility to funnel information between the boss and the employees.

> ## MISTAKE #130
> ### My Boss Drives Me Crazy Sometimes; Complaining About Him Would Make Me Feel Better
>
> It might make you feel better, but you hurt yourself in the long run. Your boss and employees will learn that you aren't loyal and they can't trust you. Even though it's tempting, it isn't a good idea.

Do you understand your boss's decisions? If not, ask for clarification, because you will have to explain these decisions to your employees. It will take more preparation to explain unpopular decisions.

### Represent Your Employees

There will be times when your boss makes decisions about your employees. You can show support for your boss by sharing important details, especially ones that will help him or her make an appropriate and informed decision. You need to pass information from your employees to your boss when needed. It's your job to filter through information, relaying what's important.

When necessary, you need to stand up to your boss and defend your employees. This will not happen often, but when it does, fully explain the situation.

## MISTAKE #131
### My Boss Is Wrong About Mark, but I Shouldn't Disagree with Him

If your boss has the wrong idea or information about a team member, it's your responsibility to supply the correct information. You need to represent your team. You know them better than your boss and need to give details to straighten out any confusion. Misunderstandings can cause problems for the employee, and it's your job to fix it.

Discuss your employees with your boss when they do something well. Your boss needs to know when employees excel. It's a great way to bring employees to your boss's attention.

# HOW TO SUPPORT YOUR BOSS

### Should You Take On Risky Projects?
Any business venture is risky. When your boss asks you to spearhead a risky project, it's normal to be concerned, but the fact that you were asked could indicate confidence in your abilities. It's a wonderful time to prove yourself. Before you accept a risky project, though, ask yourself the following questions:

- Is the project worth the risk?
- Is my team qualified to handle the project?
- Am I qualified to lead the project?
- Do we have the background and experience to do it right?

If you answered "yes" to all of these questions, then you should take on the project. If you turned down your boss at first, explain that you reconsidered the offer and are willing to take the project. If you were concerned about the project, then your team members will probably feel the same way. Be prepared to explain the situation to them.

### Be Realistic About the Risks

Underestimating the risks can cause problems. Analyze potential problems and find ways to overcome them. You cannot foresee every potential problem, but think through the project and address everything you can in the beginning.

---

### MISTAKE #132
### The Project Probably Won't Be That Bad; I Should Stop Worrying

These thoughts can lead to improper planning and can cause you many problems. You need to examine the project and be realistic about what could go wrong. Once you figure out the potential problems, find solutions for them.

---

### Prepare for Problems

Always have a Plan B. If and when there are problems, do you have other ways resolve those problems? Any time you plan a project, it is good to have a backup plan, but it's especially critical on risky projects. Proper planning and a dash of creativity can get you out of sticky situations.

### Can Other Supervisors Help?

Your boss should support you when there is a problem. After all, you make him or her look good when you succeed. Your boss can help you convey the risk and importance of the project to supervisors who are over both of you. If they truly appreciate the potential payoff, then their help can be a big asset to your team.

## MISTAKE #133
### The Supervisors Can Leave Me Hanging if I Fail

They could, but you can prevent this by preparing the project the right way. Inform your boss and his supervisors about the potential risk and the potential payoff for the company when you succeed. This can get them to rally around you and help you in case you encounter unexpected problems.

Taking on a risky project and completing it successfully is a great way to show support for your boss. There are some risky projects that can catapult your success in the company, and your boss's success as well. Make sure that you decide whether the project is worth the risk, and plan the project carefully, remembering to think about resources you'll need. Enlist the help of your team and other supervisors, always keeping the "big picture" in mind.

### Share the Workload

Have there been times when your boss came to you with problems? Maybe a department manager is out sick or behind on a project. Your boss could be in a bind and needs your help. What is your response?

## MISTAKE #134
### My Boss Asked Me to Do Someone Else's Job; I Told Him That It's Not My Job

That's not the best way to respond. Your boss may need you to do something that isn't your usual job. Ask questions to understand why he needs your help. If you want to do what the company needs, then help your boss.

What issues should you consider before you decide to accept the additional assignment? Consider that your boss needs your help and thinks you are willing to do it. He's counting on your cooperation. This could be one of the reasons you were hired for the job. Remember that managers need to be team players. When your boss is in a bind, it's a great chance to help the company. What will happen the next time you need help? The other managers and your boss may tell you "It's not my job."

You should cooperate and help your boss when needed. Are you concerned that your coworkers will take advantage of you? It is a valid concern, but there are things you can do to avoid being used. Are you truly too busy to accept more work? If so, explain your limitations to your boss.

There are times when you are needed and there aren't any other options. Review your workload to determine if anything can be postponed. Your boss may be able to help you shuffle your workload to find the time and resources for an emergency project. It's in both your best interests to make it work.

I'll end this section by telling you when it is best to refuse that additional project. Does the assignment require skills and knowledge you don't possess? If so, be honest and tell your boss that your team isn't qualified for the job. If you make a solid case and explain why you aren't the right choice, he or she should appreciate your honesty. It hurts everyone when you struggle to do something when you aren't qualified.

### Be a Team Player

A company manager needs to contribute to the overall well-being of the team. Being aggressive and driven is good, but do your supervisors think you are after their jobs? This can cause you many problems. Show them you understand your job is to help them succeed and to help the company.

## MISTAKE #135
### I Might Not Tell My Boss About Margo's Contribution

This will not make you look good. You might not get caught right away, but Margo or your boss will find out you tried to take credit for her work and you didn't recognize her work and efforts.

When your boss sees you giving credit to your employees who deserve it, he or she will learn that you are a fair person and a team player. If you share credit with your employees, then your boss won't worry that you'll take all of the credit for something your worked on to support him or her.

## MISTAKE #136
### I Deserve the Credit for This Accomplishment

Did you work extra hard on the project? Was it especially difficult? Even if these things are true, I'm sure you couldn't have done it without your boss and your team. Unless you worked on the project alone, there are other people who deserve credit. You need to recognize them for their contributions.

### Disagree in Private

Has your boss done something to make you mad? This happens, sometimes frequently. When someone makes you mad, your first inclination might be to tell the person what you think without considering who else is around. This is not acceptable behavior for an effective manager. You might see others behaving this way, but it's not the right way to handle the problem.

## MISTAKE #137
### My Boss Is Wrong; I'll Bring It Up in the Next Supervisors' Meeting

This would be a critical mistake on your part. When you have an issue with your boss, discuss the problem in private. If you complain about him or her in a meeting, it makes you look bad to everyone. When you do this kind of thing, word circulates to others within the company. This behavior can hurt you in many ways.

The same principle holds true with other team members. When you have a problem with a coworker or team member, handle that in private. It is good to make notes about the problem and what each of you said in the meeting. There will be conflicts, and as a manager, you will have to deal with these situations. You can become known as a manager who discusses problems in public or you can gain the respect of your coworkers by handling situations in private.

> ## *MISTAKE #138*
> ### *Harvey Messed Up the Project; I Need to Make an Example of Him*
>
> You might feel this will prevent others from making the same mistakes, but it will not have that effect. Team members will respect you and respond to you better when you deal with problems in private. Addressing these things in public will humiliate your employees and cause them to mistrust you.

### *Be Positive with Team Members*

Effective managers make their bosses look good. One way to be an effective manager is to encourage your team members to share ideas and suggestions. They see the department from a different perspective, and many times they can share useful suggestions. Be prepared that there will be ideas that you can't use, but occasionally they might bring you a real gem. Even when they bring you ideas that won't work, encourage and thank them for their efforts. Some of the most effective CEOs got invaluable ideas from their employees.

When a team member brings a useful suggestion to you, make a big deal of thanking them. You can express your appreciation at a team meeting. This recognizes their efforts and ideas. It also encourages others to share their ideas with you. Really good ideas should be brought to your boss's attention. Your employees will appreciate the recognition and it will motivate them to do more.

## MISTAKE #139
### There Is No Way That Idea Will Work

You may be right, but don't express it in those terms to your
employees. It's more effective to tell them you appreciate their help
and will review their suggestion. If they ask you about the idea,
tactfully let them know you will keep it for future reference.

### Tell Your Boss What Is Happening

Show your competence by handling many problems on your
own, but take time to review some more complicated problems
that you solved with your boss. It is good for your boss to know
what you can accomplish, but keep him or her notified before a
problem gets too big for you to handle. When you keep a close
eye on your projects, you will know about most problems early.

## MISTAKE #140
### There Was a Small Problem Today; I Should Tell My Boss

You don't need to bother your boss with every little issue. You were
hired to handle the easy problems. You only need to notify him or her
about the bigger problems that you cannot solve or will cause other
issues.

Here are some simple keys to keeping your boss informed and
not overwhelmed:

- Tell your boss about problems—not other team members,
  managers, or customers.

- Inform your boss before problems are out of control.

- Tell your boss about ways you found to improve some facet of the business. It may be a way to save money or to be more efficient.

## MISTAKE #141
### I Have Some Good Ideas for the Business, but Maybe I Shouldn't Tell Anyone

It is good to prepare your ideas and then present them to your boss. Your organizational skills and initiative along with your desire to help the company will be appreciated.

### Understand Why Your Boss Hired You

Why did your boss hire you? It could be your ability, loyalty commitment, and hard work. Perhaps your boss knew that you were trustworthy and would make his or her job go more smoothly.

Remember, your actions reflect on your boss. In your last job, did you have the power to make all the decisions? You are now in a different situation because you have to answer to your boss. When you make decisions, think about possible repercussions for your boss and yourself. If you support your boss and make him or her look good, then your boss will support you as well.

## MISTAKE #142
### I Made All the Decisions Before and Should Be Able to Make Them in This Position

There are jobs where one person makes the decisions, and jobs where decisions are made by groups or boards. In a large company, there is an established order about who makes the decisions. If this will be an issue, you need to discuss it before you accept the job. Established protocol isn't likely to change, and you should be prepared.

Before you begin your job, sit down with your boss to get a clear understanding of the expectations. What timeline does he or she have in mind for your training? It is good to meet with your boss each week to review your progress and expectations. If you don't get any feedback from your boss, ask for his or her thoughts on your performance. Knowing exactly what your boss needs from you will help you do your job—making his or her job easier— more effectively.

### Understand Your Boss's Job

What can your boss actually do for you? Are there certain things that aren't possible? Your boss probably does not have the ability to do everything that he or she wants. There are usually company policies and restrictions that monitor what employees can do.

Budget constraints can often limit your boss's actions. Supervisors need to submit their budget requests at a certain time of year, and it is very rare that these budget amounts are changed during the year. This could be the reason why your boss denied something you needed.

## MISTAKE #143
### My Boss Knows I Need That Equipment and There's No Reason to Deny Me

Your boss may be aware of your need, but there may be no money in the budget at the time. Is there another piece of equipment within the company that you can use? This would be a temporary solution until the new fiscal year. Mention your needs again when your boss works on the following year's budget.

Your boss must keep an eye on the overall well-being of the company. This means that you won't always get what you want. You need to understand there are times when your boss can't grant your requests. You can discuss this in the weekly meetings that I suggested. This is a good way to keep the lines of communication open between you, so you both get a chance to explain your actions. Good communication helps you to work together and to understand one another.

## When It Is Not Appropriate to Support Your Boss

You are expected to support your boss and to make him or her look good. What should you do when ethical problems arise? What is the right thing to do when your boss wants you to do something questionable, illegal, or dishonest?

### MISTAKE #144
#### My Boss Says I Have to Follow Orders; Even if They're Illegal

Your boss could threaten to fire you, but you should be able to fight that. An employer can't demand that you do something illegal or unethical. If he or she insists and you do something wrong, you're legally responsible for your actions. Would you rather find another job or be prosecuted for your actions?

If your boss is asking you to do something that you feel is wrong, evaluate why your boss is asking you to do it. Will it help the company without causing problems? Is it to make you boss look better and to hide unflattering facts? These are vastly different reasons to ask for your help. You shouldn't decide to give your support based solely on the fact that he or she is your boss.

If you aren't comfortable with an assignment, then you shouldn't be involved. You might suggest a more ethical way to handle the situation, one that will meet the same objectives without causing a moral dilemma. It's probably best, though, to protect yourself from these situations and prevent them from occurring:

- Coworkers and employers won't usually ask you to be unethical if they know you will have reservations about your involvement. When a situation arises, give solid reasons for the way you feel. Giving a weak response won't convince most people of your resolve.

- Surround yourself with honest and ethical people. Be truthful with your team about what you expect. They need to know how you want them to deal with others and to handle themselves.

- Keep thorough records of questionable things you are asked to do. Document things that others do around you and to you. You should be able to find support with upper management if there are problems with your boss, but be prepared and have solid proof before going to your boss's supervisor.

There may be times when you cannot protect yourself. The unethical behavior could be widespread. If this is the case, you may need to look for another job. Don't make a rash decision, but consider your options. Take a realistic look at the situation before you decide to leave, but understand that it is sometimes necessary.

### Show Support for Your Boss

I have worked in many capacities from peon to manager. I have found that those who are supportive and loyal to their company as well as to their boss succeed, while those who are not, do not stay with the company long.

### How to Support Your Boss

You are a worker; even if you are in management, there is still someone over you. The best policy is to be supportive of the people who are in charge. They set the policies and demand the respect. It is not easy, especially when you disagree with what is being done, but in the long run, they know more than you do. There are a few easy steps to supporting your boss: 1) Never badmouth your boss to coworkers or customers, 2) Give your boss's ideas a fair shake before you decide they stink, 3) Don't shoot your mouth off about how terrible something is before you try it; this is the best way to shoot yourself in the foot and perhaps lose your job, and 4) Respect works two ways: If you respect those above you, it will surprise you the amount of respect you will get in return.

### When It Is Not Appropriate to Support Your Boss

This is a last-ditch effort. If your boss has lost your respect and is doing things to destroy the company, you have no alternative but to withdraw your support. For example, if you are working for someone who is taking company money for personal use, these are grounds for loss of support. I'm not talking about small amounts for expenses, I'm referring to hundreds of thousands of dollars in addition to an already high salary. This is taking away from the good of the company. I'm not saying to cut off your nose to spite your face, but do keep notes of what is going on so if the time comes when an official investigation is under way, you are able to defend yourself.

Sherry Wille, Author
**www.derr-wille.com**

# PART THREE

# Building Your Team

*When you interview potential employees, keep in mind you need these people to help you accomplish your tasks and to help you look good.*

# CHAPTER 10

# Interviewing, Hiring, and Training New Employees

## EFFECTIVE INTERVIEWING

When you interview potential employees, keep in mind you need these people to help you accomplish your tasks and to help you look good. What type of people do you want to work around? What qualities are the most important to you? What types of people work well with you? These are important things to consider when you interview people and make decisions about whom you will hire.

Once you get to know your employees, pick several and ask them to make a list of what experience, background, and qualities they think are necessary to do the job. They do the job every day and would have the best idea about what helps them do it. Add your thoughts to their ideas, and file them in a safe place for use when you hire someone for the job. If you do this before you need to hire someone, you won't be in the position of not knowing what to look for in the candidates.

### Sorting the Applications

When you run an advertisement for applicants, there are many applications to review. Most managers review each and every application before deciding which people to call in for an interview.

> ## MISTAKE #145
> ### I Could Only Call in People Who Went to College
>
> It is rare that this broad approach works. Be more specific when you select the people to call. Decide what experience is needed and search for applicants with that background.

Think about your best employees. You might want to pull their applications from human resources and see what applicable background they have. If you see some consistencies, that would be a good place to start. See what they did in the past that is beneficial to the company.

I used to manage a business where we invited everyone in for interviews. This sounds unusual, but there was logic to the process. The job involved one-on-one contact with people, and we needed to see how applicants interacted with people. I called in every person with any useful skills and scheduled fifteen to twenty people at a time for group interviews.

We handed out a piece of paper and a pen to each person and asked a series of questions. Most were job related, but some were personal preferences, such as scheduling.

During the interviews, I made notes about applicants' interaction and behavior with the other applicants. We thought about the candidates overnight and discussed them the next morning. We then called in three or four applicants for face-to-face interviews. By that time we had a good idea about the applicants, and we could personalize the interviews. It was an unusual technique, but it allowed us to watch the applicants interact with other people—something that you don't see when you talk with them individually. There may be alternative ways to use this technique in your department.

## MISTAKE #146
### I'll Call in Everyone and Watch Them; That's Better Than Wasting Time with Their Applications

It's never a waste of time to review the applications. The applications contain valuable information that you need about their backgrounds. From that point, narrow down the list even further.

Before you receive a pile of applications, make a list of the qualities the "perfect" applicant needs. What experience and background do you want? You need to have a clear picture of the employee you are looking for. Once you have that in your mind, begin to review the applications that were submitted.

## MISTAKE #147
### I Won't Prepare for My First Interviews; I'll Know the Right Person

This could be a waste of your time and the interviewees' time. Another big problem is that you appear unprofessional to potential employees. Even if you find a qualified applicant, he or she may not want to work for a boss who is unprepared. Savvy applicants interview you too, and can decide whether or not to work with you.

When I review applications, I make three piles: 1) ones to interview, 2) ones to possibly interview, and 3) people who aren't qualified. My criteria include:

### Definitely Interview

These people have the background and experience that the position requires. The interview will help you determine if the applicants have the personality and attitude you need.

### Possibly Interview

These people have some of the background and experience you

## MISTAKE #148
### These People Don't Have the Right Background, so I Won't Consider Them

Other experience could make someone a qualified applicant. If there is anything on the application that draws your attention, consider the applicant. On the flip side, if there is something that proves someone is wrong for the job, you shouldn't consider him or her.

need, and you want to learn more. Personality and attitude could be a deciding factor with these applicants.

### Don't Interview

Many people apply for jobs that they simply are not qualified to do. That will be your third pile. You can tell by reviewing their work history that they don't have the background you need.

Once you have three piles, focus on the first two and determine who has the background and experience you need. Other factors that will help you to narrow down your search will depend on

## MISTAKE #149
### I Have to Interview Applicants in a Private Room

It's good to discuss personal information in private, but you can explain the details of the job in a public setting. For some jobs, that might be the best approach. Use your discretion about what parts of your interview to conduct in the actual work area.

your application's questions. If your boss and supervisors will let you, make changes to the application and tailor it to your needs.

Another technique I used was to interview prospective employees in our workroom during a reasonably busy time of day. It could be an intimidating atmosphere, and I needed to see if they could handle that. The area was compact and we worked around each other every day. People who wanted a solitary workspace would never survive on the floor. Some applicants' discomfort was obvious, but others seemed able to work around the activity. The job also involved pulling supplies and restocking carts. Accuracy and speed were critical. During our interview, I asked applicants to help me with my inventory sheet. I noticed whether they wanted to chat or if they focused on pulling the supplies accurately. I was happy with most of the people I hired in that position. Interviews hadn't been done that way before, but it helped me to determine if the applicants would focus on the things that I felt were important.

### Talking to Applicants

When you decide which applicants you want to meet, decide how to conduct the interviews. Make sure to describe the job in

> ## MISTAKE #150
> ### The Applicant Cringed When I Explained the Job Details, but Her Experience Is Great
>
> No matter how good the experience is, if an applicant cringes, he or she isn't an ideal candidate. When you explain the job details, watch applicants' reactions to see if they're really interested. Do they just need a job, or are they really interested in THIS job? You will learn to tell the difference.

detail. Sometimes a better understanding of the job will convince the applicants that they aren't interested.

Start with a quick overview of the job. You need to explain the job title, the duties involved, how the position fits into the "big picture" of the business, and the typical working conditions.

Be honest about the negative aspects of the job. Painting a rosy picture won't help anyone. If you give applicants an unrealistic idea of the job, they won't be happy when you hire them. Your goal should be to find the best possible fit for the position you need to fill. You can only do this if you are honest with the interviewees. Are there unusual hours or night shifts? Will they need to work outside? Are there uncomfortable working conditions?

## MISTAKE #151
### The Applicants Won't Like the Hours. I Won't Tell Them About the Night Shifts

Applicants always remember the things you want them to forget. You lose credibility when they discover you didn't tell them the truth.

I was supervisor in one job where we didn't have any windows and only two solid doors. Claustrophobic people would have a problem with this situation. Another job involved working near 400-degree ovens. There were people who couldn't work around the intense heat. These things may not seem like a big deal to you, but you need to explain them to applicants. Don't scare them, but be realistic.

## MISTAKE #152
### I Want to See if This Person Is Hardy, so I'll Scare Him

That isn't a good test. You can be honest and give interviewees the details without scaring them unnecessarily.

At one job, all of my employees were college students. The job required them to work Friday and Saturday nights. Some people had to work during the Super Bowl, and some worked during campus events. I worked hard to schedule them fairly. I needed one employee to be "on call" each Friday and Saturday night. This required that they not drink. I gave them a simple bonus for being on call. If I called them in, they had to be sober and able to drive. They knew this in the beginning, and I never had a problem.

If the applicant is still interested after you explain the job thoroughly, you can discuss the benefits. Mention the starting pay, holiday and vacation policies, and any other benefits the job offers. Be careful not to make promises about pay raises, time off, and other things you cannot control at that point.

Your interviews shouldn't feel like an inquisition. When you ask questions, leave them open-ended. Use questions that begin with who, what, when, where, why, and how. Key things you need to determine include details about their education, work experience, attendance record, and the reasons why they left their last jobs.

## MISTAKE #153
### I Don't Need to Tell Them About the Job Benefits

If you are interested in hiring the person, tell them the good and bad aspects of the job. Once they are hired, they will discuss these things with coworkers and may wonder why you kept information from them. This is another way to lose credibility with new employees.

## MISTAKE #154
### I Think the Interviewee Is Hiding Something; I'll Ask Pointed Questions

This will only put the person on the defensive. You can get more details without being confrontational. If you think that someone is hiding something big, then you probably don't want that person.

Some great questions that can help you get into the applicant's mind include the following:

- What type of job do you picture yourself in at this time in your life? Why would you pick that job? What have you done that makes you qualified for that position?

- Who was your best supervisor? What made them a great boss? Do you have any of these qualities? How could a manager improve on the things your ideal boss did?

- Who was your worst supervisor? Why? Do you have similar qualities? How would you overcome these qualities?

The applicant might not have answers for all of your questions. Questions like these make the person look inside themselves and will give you insights into the sort of boss and situation with which he or she works best. Are you that type of boss? It should give you insights into whether you can work together.

## Questions You Cannot Ask an Applicant

There are legal guidelines on what you cannot ask applicants, including the following:

- Race and/or national origin
- Religion
- Sex
- Age
- Marital status
- Disabilities
- Criminal record
- Physical abilities

You cannot legally ask these questions, but many of the answers will be obvious. Many disabilities are evident during interviews. The only reason to be concerned about these issues is if it would prevent the applicant from doing the job. Otherwise, you cannot eliminate them because of this. Physical abilities are similar. Tread carefully around these situations. If in doubt, seek legal advice prior to interviewing.

## MISTAKE #155
### I Need to Know if the Interviewee Has a Criminal Record, So I Can Ask This One Time

That would be breaking the law. The government is very strict about what you can and cannot ask an applicant. If it's a big concern, delete the applicant from your list.

When you interview people, focus on positive things. These include experiences that fit into the job requirements. Have they done similar work in the past? What key characteristics do they exhibit that are suited for your position? Some of these traits include:

- Achievements
- Job attendance
- Attitude
- Physical condition
- Energy and enthusiasm
- Pays attention when you talk

### Make Interviews More Successful

Everyone is nervous during an interview, but try to put interviewees at ease. Don't make notes during the interview. The person you're interviewing might be distracted, so try to make mental notes during the interview, and then make written notes afterwards while everything is still fresh in your mind.

Paint a realistic picture of what the job entails and what is required of the potential employee. Be honest about the education and experience that you want. During the interview, it's better to leave the applicant's personal life out of the process. If an applicant mentions his or her children or spouse, then you can pursue it. While you were talking, did you notice inconsistencies in the applicant's story? He or she may just be nervous, but follow up on these things and ask for specifics. Practice keeping your expression and tone even during interviews. Even if you hear something that shocks you, try not to show your surprise.

It is tempting to rush interviews, especially when other people are scheduled. There is no doubt that you have plenty of work to do, but don't make the person feel rushed. If you glance at your watch, the interviewee may shut down and the rest of the interview won't be productive. Give the conversation your undivided attention and take your time.

## MISTAKE #156
### I Have Five More Interviews so I Need to Rush Through Them

Your employees will be a key factor in your success or failure, and you need to get to know the applicants in order to make a sound decision. The interviews need to stay on schedule, but try not to rush through them. If you get a negative feeling about an applicant, then you can move it along. However, if you feel good about an applicant, spend time learning his or her qualifications.

## EFFECTIVE HIRING

Once you decide what you need in an employee, you can make a final selection. Be certain about the education and experience that you want, because bad hiring decisions can cost time, effort, and money.

## MISTAKE #157
### I Just Need to Fill This Position with Someone

That attitude will not serve you well. Turnover takes time and effort. It's better to thoroughly screen the applicants to make an informed decision. Your department runs better with a complete and qualified team.

### Reduce Potential Turnover

Effective hiring is a great way to reduce potential turnover. Thinking carefully about what you're looking for in an employee and conducting great interviews will help make the right hiring decision. When people are unhappy in a job, there is a higher chance of tardiness and low-quality work. It's hard to be enthusiastic about a job that you dislike. When you aren't happy, it's difficult to give your best.

Do you think that it costs the business money when you hire the wrong person? The U.S. Department of Labor says, "A bad hire will cost a company the equivalent of that employee's salary for a six-month period." When managers consider this, they only figure the person's payroll. When you think about turnover, consider what it actually costs the department. These expenses should be included in your calculations:

- Possible overtime to get the necessary work done.

- Your time to review applications and conduct interviews.

- Any people who are training employees will be at lower productivity.

High employee turnover is something your boss and supervisors are concerned about. Your team members are required to do additional work while there aren't enough qualified people in the department. It is also discouraging to the people who train the new hires. Training is difficult and their work falls further behind.

When you review applications, search for the experience and personalities that fit in with the company, and then sort out the people who fit the job. But remember that qualifications and experience aren't the only things to consider.

Southwest Airlines takes this to a whole different level. The company's hiring policies are a little unorthodox. They hire people based on their attitude. A person with less experience and a better attitude will usually be hired instead of a person who has experience, but a poor attitude. Employees can be trained to do their jobs, but attitude is harder to change. The traits that Southwest Airlines looks for are "team spirit, cheerfulness, optimism, decision-making ability, communication, self-confidence, and self-starter skills."

## MISTAKE #158
### I Don't Remember Her Name, But I Want to Hire the Perky Blonde

While she might help the office aesthetics, her appearance does not guarantee that she can do the job. Evaluate the qualifications of the applicants and keep in mind the personality traits that you want to work around. Pleasant, optimistic self-starters are helpful on a team.

## MISTAKE #159
### Any Type of Test Should Be All Right

If you plan to give prospective employees a test, it is more helpful to give them a test that reveals the qualities you want. A random test might not help you find the results you need. There are enough tests available to find one that works for your department.

Some companies test potential employees. There are many tests that you can use. If you plan to do this, find tests that give results pertaining to qualities your employees need. Also, find tests that are easy to understand. Many people simply cannot take tests; this could skew your results. You may find that the tests don't get the results you want. If this is the case, change the tests or stop using them.

When you review your interview notes, don't ignore your gut feelings. Sometimes we get a good or bad feeling about a person. If your feelings were right in the past, you should pay attention to them. Some people have great intuition and they should listen to these feelings.

## MISTAKE #160
### I'm Not Sure Which Qualities I Need

That can be a common concern. A good way to figure this out is by considering your best employees. Think of each one and note which qualities help you. Make a list of these qualities and see which ones are repeated; these are the qualities you need in potential employees.

Keep your list of qualities and qualifications handy when you are making your final decisions. Decide which qualities are more important to you. Some will be critical, while others are helpful but not necessary. It is best to have them clearly in mind before you make any final decisions.

Every application I've ever completed or used for applicants has a section for references. It is a standard thing that people always ask. This is ironic, since personal references are basically useless. In the 20 years I've been conducting interviews, only one person listed an acquaintance that didn't like him and told me how awful he was.

On the other hand, business references are critical. Be sure the applicant supplies business references and check them. Legally, references can't tell you a lot, but they can give you a sense of a person. These are some of the things you can learn about applicants through their business references:

- The position they held
- What their responsibilities were
- Their rate of pay
- How long they worked there
- Their attendance record
- Why they left the job

Checking references will give you the chance to verify the information the applicant gave you and the impressions you have about them. I've called many references and have gotten a good sense about potential employees, even when they couldn't directly answer my questions. I've heard it said many times that anyone who hires without checking references is crazy. It's a simple way to learn more about the applicant that managers should always utilize.

## EFFECTIVE TRAINING

You made the decision and offered the job to the candidate you prefer. If the first candidate didn't accept the job, then go to the next application that you like. It might take a few calls to find a person who accepts the job, but don't let that discourage you.

Once you hire someone, you need to train him or her. How do you help this person get started? Keep in mind that a new

### MISTAKE #161
#### We Could Have a Big Party to Say "Welcome to the Department"

That might be over the top and embarrassing to a new person. Until the team gets to know the new person, it's better to keep it low-key.

employee's training will make a big difference in his or her performance. You need to start new employees off right.

Your first priority is to put the new employee at ease. I always told my team when new employees would be starting, and there were people I counted on to make them feel welcome. Don't overwhelm a new team member on the first day.

How did you feel on your first day? Were you overwhelmed? Did you want to run out the door? Your new employee is probably feeling all of these things. Think of things that would make a first

### MISTAKE #162
#### There's a Lot of Information to Cover on the First Day; I Hope the New Person Remembers Everything

The first day is overwhelming and there is a lot to absorb. At one job, I gave each new employee a note pad and pen to make notes. They would need it for other things, but it was a nice touch during the first week.

day better; these are the things you need to do for new employees.

Give a quick tour on the first day to help new employees get settled. Introduce new coworkers. At one job, I handed out name tags that we wore during the first week to help new people learn our names. People won't remember everything from their first day, so don't overload them with information.

The new employee needs information about the workweek, lunch breaks, how to submit time cards, and how to collect paychecks. This will lead into how scheduling, sick days, and vacation works.

After the new employee has toured the department and met their coworkers, review what the job involves. This gives a reference point for the details you share. Be sure to mention that you will be available when he or she has questions. New employees need to know you won't abandon them.

## MISTAKE #163
### I Should Start a Rotation and Let Everyone Take Turns Training People

Training requires special skills and abilities. Some employees aren't qualified to train and some won't want to be trainers. This is probably for the best. Don't push people who don't want to train new employees. They would be in a bad frame of mind to train if you force them.

Give careful consideration about who will train the new team member. This should be arranged ahead of time, and the trainer needs to be ready on the first day. Good trainers are usually:

- Patient

- Detail-oriented

- Well trained, competent, and familiar with all aspects of the job

- Positive about the department and company

- Willing to train a new employee

- Understanding that more than a minimal effort is needed

Once you turn the new employee over to his or her trainer, follow up often. It's good to schedule meetings with new employees each day for the first couple of weeks. These meetings allow you to discuss concerns or questions. You can also use these times to evaluate their progress.

It's good to start new employees out with simple projects, but you need to add more challenges. Don't overwhelm them with too much too soon, but keep them challenged and don't let them get bored. All of these things help them become strong members of the team.

# CHAPTER 11

# Managing People

## HOW TO BE A BETTER BOSS

You're getting settled into your new job; you know how to interview, hire, and train new employees. Now we need to discuss how to become a better boss. Following a simple list isn't enough to make you a better manager, but I'll share some basic management principles to help you hone your skills and become more effective.

### MISTAKE #164
#### I Have a To-Do List for Managers; That Should Be Enough

"Should be" isn't good enough for you. You need to put the principles into practice and show you have the right attitude by treating your team members fairly and with respect. It isn't fair to expect more from them than you are willing to give. Implement these ideas from the start and you will get better over time.

We discussed some of these principles earlier, but you are at a different place in your training now. These points will make you a more effective manager and help your team members respect you and work with you better.

When employees complain, handle the problems quickly. Show your team members that you are concerned about things that make their job more difficult. Find ways to keep morale high and show your team that you care.

## MISTAKE #165
### My Employees Want Changes, but They Can Wait

If the changes are within your power, make them happen. It's easier to ignore the requests, but this causes problems with your team members. Find ways to improve conditions for your team. When they come to you with suggestions and requests, do everything you can to help them.

There are a hundred little things each day, but don't let them distract you from the important things that you must handle. I'm not talking about serious problems, but the small irritations. It could be silly things your team members do that drive you crazy or routine tasks that you must do.

## MISTAKE #166
### The Little Things Require All My Attention

There are many small things to handle every day. Find a way to manage them. They can overwhelm you if you don't get a handle on them. You will learn to identify little things, but the big things need your attention first.

Keep an eye on the details within your department. When you watch the little things, you can keep them from becoming big problems. Some people like to ignore the little things and hope they will go away. They don't go away, but they often become bigger problems. One good example is when your office equipment begins to have problems. Preventative maintenance is a great way to handle problems while they are small. When employees bring things to you, take a look to see if they require your attention.

There are unpleasant things every manager needs to do, and many need to be done every day. I like to get the difficult or irritating things done first. Then I can look forward to the more enjoyable tasks. Some tasks might have deadlines that you must meet. Remember that official tasks with deadlines may also come with penalties and fines if you don't complete them on time. It's easier to tackle these when they land on your desk. Then when they are completed, you can forget about them.

## MISTAKE #167
### Why Do I Need to Trust My Employees?

Trust is critical in any department. Your employees need to feel they can trust you to look out for their interests. In turn, you need to trust your team members. This gives you greater peace of mind when you are busy with other things. You can't watch your team every minute of the day, so you need to trust them to do a good job.

Do you trust your team members? Are they qualified to handle their jobs? It's critical that you trust them. If you aren't confident about some members of your team, you need to find a way to increase your confidence. Would some additional or specialized training help you feel better about their abilities? You should look into these options.

## MISTAKE #168
### I Look Foolish; Maybe I Should Give Up

Everyone looks foolish at times. This is especially true when you are relatively new to a job. It takes time to learn new things. Remember the old saying, "To err is human…" It is normal to make mistakes, and as you learn more, you will make fewer of them.

Don't focus on your mistakes. Everyone makes them, so learn from them and move ahead. If others in the department want to harp on them, try to laugh about it and move on. Keep in mind that most mistakes are small. The important thing is to learn from your mistakes.

There will be times when people within your department and the company will offer you help. Don't take their help for granted, and do show your appreciation. As you gain more experience and knowledge about the job, you still need to reassure your team that you appreciate their help.

How do you handle it when people come to you with ideas and suggestions? Do you shrug them off or do you listen? It's hard to know who will have winning suggestions, so you need to follow up on your team members' ideas.

## MISTAKE #169
### I Don't Have Time to Be Bothered with My Employees' Ideas

You need to find time to listen when they have suggestions. It is important to your employees that you listen to them and show you care. It is possible that an employee will make a wonderful suggestion. Keep your ears and mind open when employees have something to share.

We can learn more about listening to employees from Bill Gates. He believes every employee has something to contribute. I learned that Bill Gates didn't gravitate toward the Internet until one of his employees noticed that Cornell students used the Internet for more than research and then brought the information back to his employer. If he hadn't felt comfortable sharing his ideas, where would Bill Gates be today? He might still be rich, but he would've missed an incredible opportunity.

Is your confidence evident to others in the company? Are you obnoxious about your abilities or are you tactful and respectful of others? I had an assistant manager who walked in the door with the belief that he was better than everyone. It was a difficult attitude to deal with on a daily basis. Younger employees may respond to this for a short time, but your experienced team members will get tired of this behavior quickly. Quiet and assured confidence is a more effective way to get the job done and maintain the respect of your team.

## MISTAKE #170
### I'm Confident in My Skills, so I'm an Overconfident Manager

There are managers who use that technique. Ask yourself something: Do you respond well to that management style? Most people don't respond to obnoxious managers. Show your team members you are confident in your abilities without being rude. This is a more effective way to do business.

Are you a moody person? Men and women can both be moody at times and for various reasons. Whether you've had a bad day or something more critical has happened, keep your personal life and problems out of the workplace. I won't say it's easy, because it's not. But it is critical for an effective and professional manager. I managed an office for a man who liked to talk with clients about problems with his girlfriend. This might have made him feel better, but it undermined his professionalism. When people ask how you are, you don't need to elaborate.

A key principle is to be happy in your job. If you dread your job each day, you need to make changes. Make changes and adjustments, and then decide if you are still unhappy. You need to find a way to tolerate your job, or it's time for a change. I suggest that you find another job before you leave your current job. No matter how unhappy you are, don't leave without somewhere to go.

## MISTAKE #171
### I'm Just Not Happy; Maybe I Should Quit

In your first management position, you will feel overwhelmed. Take time to settle into the job. From personal experience, I can tell you that it almost always gets better. Look for changes that will make the situation better for you.

### Team Members Should Work with You, Not Against You

The simplest way to get cooperation from your employees is to gain their respect. When your team members respect and trust you, they will work harder for you. There are a few basic things that will make this easier for you:

- Treat your team members fairly.

- Defend your team members when they need your support.

- Be nice. That seems simple, but it's not always easy.

- Let your team voice their thoughts about decisions in your department.

- Exercise as much flexibility as you can.

Do these things from the first day you arrive. You will learn more about your team and will improve over time. Keep your eyes open for team members who want to take advantage of you. When your team members see someone trying to use you, they will support you if you treat them well.

Some new managers want to use fear since they have management power. This gains short-term benefits, but it isn't an effective way to manage your department or to gain respect from your team members. Treat your employees fairly and they will respond better.

When you deal with employees, be consistent. It isn't always easy, but make the effort. This gives you credibility with your team. If you are inconsistent, your credibility will suffer. If you must treat two people differently, explain why it needs to be handled that way. This shows your team members they can trust you.

# BE THEIR BOSS, NOT THEIR FRIEND

The department manager shouldn't socialize with his or her employees. This isn't meant to be cruel, just practical. Employees need to be reprimanded at times, and it's hard to discipline your friends. It is also possible that others in the department will accuse you of showing favoritism. These things cause problems in the department and can lower team morale.

> ## MISTAKE #172
> ### My Employees Know That Our Relationship at Work Is All Business
>
> When a manager spends time outside work with his or her employees, it is easy for everyone to be confused. Employees conveniently forget you're the manager when there is a problem. Any friendship between you and employees can cloud the real issues and promote problems within the department.

The longer you work with the people in your department, the more likely that you could become friends. You need to keep a reasonable distance. I'm not suggesting that you be cold to anyone, but avoid being too friendly. There will be times when you have to make tough decisions, and that is hard to do when you deal with friends.

It is possible to be a friendly boss, but draw the line at socializing outside of work. When employees ask you to go out, you need to turn them down in a kind and tactful way. This is much harder to do once you begin socializing, so it's better not to start this practice.

## MISTAKE #173
### I'll Go Out with Them on Friday Nights, but No Other Time

That is a bad idea. It would be much better for you to find other people to socialize with. Your Friday-night activities could be mentioned in the department on Monday, causing bad feelings with other employees.

When your employees spend time with you, they can have difficulty remembering you are in charge. They will see you as a friend, not a boss, and that causes problems when you need to discipline them. It takes practice to walk the line between friend and boss, but an effective manager needs to stay on the right side of the line.

There will be company-sponsored events that you need to attend. These can include parties, picnics, banquets, and similar activities. This is an opportunity to get to know people within the company in a more relaxed situation.

## MISTAKE #174
### I Should Avoid the Company Banquet

Company picnics, banquets, and parties are events you need to attend; these are business events. Keep in mind that you are a manager and need to maintain proper behavior. If you have questions about what is expected, talk with your boss before the event.

Keep an eye out for people who might drink too much at company events. It is better to stay away from people who are drunk. That is much better than getting involved and making the situation escalate. Remember not to drink too much yourself—as a manager you need to set an example.

It's good to have firm rules for your behavior. When you decide whether to do something, remember this comment: "Never do anything with an employee that you wouldn't do with your firm's number-one client or customer." You could use this when you decide how to behave with an employee. Team members should be treated with the same respect that you show a client. Don't do things that show a lack of respect for clients or employees. If you are in doubt, don't do it.

## MISTAKE #175
### My Behavior Might Embarrass Someone Else, but My Team Members Know Me

There are two major problems with that comment. First, your team shouldn't know you like that. Second, respect yourself and your employees enough to maintain acceptable behavior.

### Don't Get Too Close, but Don't Be Cold

Managers have to learn to communicate with their employees. We will discuss how to communicate effectively in Chapter 17. Share friendly talk and instructions with your team members, but don't get too friendly. If you cross the line, some employees could become resentful. When you make assignments, dispense discipline, or complete performance evaluations, you could be accused of showing favoritism. Some employees will complain no matter how you deal with them, but this situation gives them more ammunition to use against you.

## MISTAKE #176
### This Is a Bad Task and I Shouldn't Assign It to the Employee Who Is My Friend

This is a prime reason why you shouldn't become friendly with your team members. It could be seen as favoritism and would start problems within the department. Other employees could complain to your boss, causing problems for you and your friend.

If you become too close to your employees, they may challenge your decisions and instructions. When a manager makes assignments, employees need to follow through with them. This helps the department to run smoothly. Employees who disagree can stir up problems for the manager. This can cause you to lose credibility within the department.

## MISTAKE #177
### My Other Employees Are Teasing My Friends

This is the same mentality as teasing a teacher's pet. It might be innocent or it could be resentment. Either motivation can cause rifts within the department.

Have you noticed that coworkers tease employees who are friends with their supervisors? This is similar to the way a teacher's pet is treated in school. When you show favoritism to your employees, it leaves them open to harassment from other team members.

When you become friendly with some employees, this can cause divisions within your team. The employees who aren't being singled out for additional attention can start problems for you or the favored employees. Isn't there enough to contend with on a normal day? Avoid being overly friendly with your team members, and you will avoid additional problems.

### Don't Show Favoritism

At times a manager is asked to choose employees to receive recognition for doing their job well. Some team members will never be recognized, which can cause resentment. This is especially true when these employees can accuse you of showing favoritism. Is there anything in the way you treat your team members which would appear improper? You can avoid these problems by treating your team members consistently.

Some companies only recognize the overachievers. Is there something you can do to recognize other employees who excel but who aren't your top performers? You could have a bulletin board to feature these employees or offer gift certificates or something similar for employees who do a good job. They will appreciate the recognition and it may help some of the resentment when they don't receive top-performance awards.

> ## MISTAKE #178
> ### The Company Only Recognizes the Top Performers; That's Good Enough
>
> If the company doesn't recognize the other good people in the department, find a way to do it yourself. Show your appreciation to team members who work hard, even when they aren't recognized by the company.

Take time on a regular basis to thank your employees. Each team member who does a good job should know they are appreciated. You might have a pizza party for your team members from time to time. This could coordinate with completion of an especially difficult project. When complicated projects are completed, there are usually a number of people who deserve your appreciation. Find simple ways to show your entire team that you appreciate their effort.

### Be Firm but Fair

Every manager needs to understand that there are times when employees complain. It is a rule of business that you cannot avoid. There are times when you have to insist that the employees do their jobs. They might not want to, but that isn't the point. They were hired for a job and they need to do it.

There could be a variety of reasons why employees complain. They could think that you're pushing an undesirable job on them. There are some tasks that no one wants to do, but someone has to complete them or you have to explain the problem to management.

## MISTAKE #179
### I'll Tell My Boss That My Team Refused the Project

I would like to hear your boss's response to that. He won't care that the team would prefer to not do it. It's your job to get it done. That is a simple statement, but that doesn't mean it will always be easy. This is another reason why you need to be above reproach and to maintain control of your team.

Remember that it's your responsibility to get the job done. That means someone has to do every project. At times your department will be assigned undesirable projects, but they still need to be done. You may need to be firm with your employees to get the work completed, but you shouldn't be harsh.

Your team members cannot set the schedule and agenda for your department. That's one of your responsibilities. When you don't assign tasks properly, the department can become chaotic. This isn't in anyone's best interests, so you need to stay in control.

Have you noticed how irritating it is when low-producing employees complain about their work assignments? It's easier to accept complaints and suggestions from the star workers in your department. When low-performing team members register a complaint, take time to evaluate if they have a basis for the complaint. If they do, how can you remedy the situation? Many times, their complaints are caused by their personal situations, not you or the department. Try to find out why they are complaining without getting too involved. It's not your responsibility to be their priest or psychiatrist. If you discover something serious, suggest they get help.

Watch when the same people tell you repeatedly they are too busy for a new project. Keep an eye on them and see if they refuse certain types of projects. Other employees will notice this and it can create frustration and lower morale in the department.

## MISTAKE #180
### I Asked Judy to Work on a Difficult Project, but She Is Still Busy with Another Job

Does this happen with Judy often? If it does, start looking at her work more closely. Are there specific types of projects she turns down? If so, you have to become more insistent. It could be a ploy to avoid hard projects, and you need to put an end to this behavior.

Each of these things makes a difference in how your department functions. You should not allow any indication of impropriety because it will cause problems for you, your employees, and the department as a whole. You are the manager and you need to maintain an effective and positive team.

I was a credit manager for a large oil company. I applied for that position, took an IQ test, spoke with a physiologist, and had multiple interviews. I passed everything and was offered the job at only 23 years old.

When I arrived at the job, I was the youngest person working in the office and the boss of some of the people. At first I had a lot of trouble because of my age; I had to prove myself through my job and how I performed it. There were always the problems because of my age and being new. Once I had been there for a while, the younger people (older than me) started to accept me, because I was fair, did a great job, was nice, and tried hard.

I have never had a problem separating friendship from my career. I think being in collections helped me separate friendship from business. I had to have meetings to explain to my employees that we were there to work, do a good job, and we needed to work together. We could have lunch or see each other socially, but that was separate from our time at work. Most of them did not understand this, though my meeting did help. The girls who worked for me hadn't thought about being friends with their boss. Some of them expected special treatment because we had lunch together. I explained to them that we are there to work and not to make friends. My first priority was my job, their job, and both of us complementing each other.

My advice is to have a meeting with your employees and explain this to them. Most don't think about separating work from friendship.

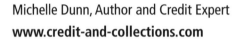

Explaining this will help things flow smoother and you can do a great job and get along. Always put your work first, do it well, and help them do their jobs in any way you can. Offer support and encouragement; be honest, helpful and courteous; and always be professional. Some of these things depend on the person, but a lot depends on how you handle the situation.

Michelle Dunn, Author and Credit Expert
**www.credit-and-collections.com**

# CHAPTER 12

# Building a Positive Work Environment

A manager's job includes resolving complaints and problems. These issues can hinder productivity in your department and they need to be handled promptly. Show your support by listening to your team members and acting on their complaints. Try to see the situation from your employees' point of view. If it is warranted, will you make the necessary changes?

## MISTAKE #181
### Helen Mentioned a Problem, But I Don't Have Time to Deal with It

You need to make time. This could include talking to Helen briefly to get the details. It might mean looking into her complaint to see if it's valid. If it is a valid complaint, you'll have to act on it.

Make necessary decisions in a timely manner. If you procrastinate, the situation will get worse and dissatisfaction could spread through the department. There are times when you need additional time to find the appropriate solution. Let the employees know that you are working on the situation but need time to find the best resolution.

## MISTAKE #182
### Elsa Is Right That We Need Better Lighting, but It Has to Wait

Is the delay caused by a budget constraint? Explain that to Elsa. Do you have another good reason to delay? If there isn't a good reason, then do everything in your power to resolve the problem. Lighting is critical to doing a job. Talk with the maintenance person about a time frame to fix this. Move quickly on complaints that you can solve.

It's better to keep your eyes open for potential problems and try to prevent them. When you get to know the employees and the company, you may be able to stop things before they cause complaints. Here are some tips to help you deal with potential complaints before they get worse.

- Consider the actual complaint and not the person who is complaining. The complaint could be valid, but your judgment can be clouded by the person who brings the situation to your attention.

## MISTAKE #183
### The Complaint Sounds Valid, but She Is a Chronic Complainer

Even if the employee is a chronic complainer, look into the problem. If you find there is a situation, do what is necessary to fix the problem. Just because someone likes to complain, that doesn't mean he or she is never right.

- Offer consistent feedback to your employees about how they are doing on their jobs. This shows your interest and they could give you input on things that make their job more difficult.

- Some people almost never complain. When they mention a problem, you should pay attention to them. It's usually a valid problem.

- Accept constructive suggestions from team members, your boss, and others who are familiar with your department.

## MISTAKE #184
### Who Does She Think She Is to Tell Me That I'm Wrong?

Even if a comment wasn't stated tactfully, consider the comment. Is there a better way to perform your duties? At times, employees may have invaluable input for you. Think about the essence of what was said and see if they have a valid point.

- When you notice irritants in your department, find ways to eliminate these potential problems. Irritants can become obstacles to your team.

- Be careful not to impulsively make promises that you cannot keep. Some things are out of your control. Other things aren't your job.

## MISTAKE #185
### I'll Make This Promise Even Though It's My Boss's Responsibility

I learned long ago not to make promises I can't deliver. Mention the situation to the person who is responsible for that duty; he or she will decide what to do.

- Get a clear picture of the problem and make a prompt decision. Make the decision after you have all the facts. Your team members want a quick decision, but don't be in a rush to decide before you have all the facts.

- When you hear gossip within the department, stay out of it. Employees can use this against you when a situation escalates.

## MISTAKE #186
### There Is Such Great Gossip in This Department

It may be tempting to be involved in the departmental gossip, but this will undermine the positive things you have accomplished. It can be used against you when there are conflicts or problems within the department.

- When you have a resolution to a departmental problem, make an announcement. However, if the solution involves disciplining a team member, handle that in private.

- There could be times when team members have a problem with company policies. When this happens, take the complaint to your boss. He or she might be able to fix the problem or talk to a supervisor who can look into it.

## MISTAKE #187
### My Team Has a Problem with a Company Policy, and I Agree with Them

Changing company policy isn't your job. Discuss the concerns with your boss, but don't tell your team members that you agree. It's better to stay neutral and let the supervisors handle the problem.

# DEALING WITH COMPLAINTS

There will always be complaints in a business situation. Many times, these are insignificant, but you still need to look into the details in case it's a real problem.

Keep in mind that no one can resolve every problem. When you are faced with complaints, consider the following questions:

- Is there any substance to the complaints?

- How can I satisfy the employee?

- Is a change needed within the department?

- Did a recent change in the department cause the complaint?

When you are the new manager, you are a good target for complaints. Existing employees might take the chance to recycle old complaints, hoping that you will resolve them. You might ask your boss if some of these complaints were brought to his or her attention before.

## MISTAKE #188
### I'm Not Responding to These Old Complaints

The employees may see you as a way to get their complaints resolved. Take a few minutes to listen to the complaint and see if their complaint is justified. If so, you need to take action, and if not, tactfully let them know that it's not possible.

It's important to check into each complaint, but tactfully dismiss them if they're invalid. Learn to distinguish between critical problems and frivolous complaints. If the problems seem unfounded, you might ask for more details. Have a clear picture before you decide whether to act on a complaint or not.

There will be times when your team members want the latest equipment that contains all the "bells and whistles." This isn't necessary unless there are serious problems with the existing equipment. Most machinery and equipment problems can be repaired.

---

### MISTAKE #189
#### My Team Members Want New Equipment; I'll Just Submit a Request

Talk to your maintenance crew and ask what the equipment needs. If there's a big problem, then submit a request. Your maintenance crew can usually find a way to fix the existing machines, at least temporarily.

---

Replacing these things can be extremely expensive and could be outside the budgetary restraints of the department and company at the time. When team members bring these things to your attention, explain why it isn't necessary or possible. Let them know their request can be reviewed when the next department budget is compiled. Be careful not to promise anything; the final decision on large purchases is probably not within the scope of your job.

Complaints that will hamper productivity need to be a top priority. Another priority should be safety concerns. Both of these issues can cause many problems and need to be addressed quickly. Your boss will be interested in things that impact productivity and safety.

---

### MISTAKE #190
#### My Workers Should Be Able to Do Their Jobs Even with This Faulty Equipment

Things that keep people from doing their work need your immediate attention. Repair or replace broken equipment.

---

One way to make sure your equipment stays in good repair is to have a good relationship with the maintenance staff. In most businesses, they are overworked and have to decide whom to help first. Your department can get better treatment and service if you treat the repair crew with respect. Their friendship and effort can help you extend the life of your equipment.

## MISTAKE #191
### I Need to Rearrange the Workspace Soon

You need to learn the job and know the employees before you change things. Once you know the situation better, you can make effective recommendations for change. If you make changes too soon, your employees are sure to be unhappy.

New managers sometimes have an impulse to rearrange the department. Get to know the employees and the department before you try to change things. You should be aware that rearranging people or equipment usually causes more complaints than it eliminates. If you are determined to make changes, explain why they are necessary and ask for employees' input. Helping your team members understand your reasoning could alleviate some of the complaints.

### Handle Chronic Complainers
It can be hard to identify chronic complainers when you are new to the job. Over time, you will know them well. Sometimes there are no solutions for a problem. Chronic complainers don't like to hear that. They want to see a resolution to their concerns, but explain that some things can't be done. Prepare for this conversation by researching the situation before you say it can't be resolved.

Is there an underlying reason for their complaints? They may want more attention. It will help if you are kind to them, but you need to establish limits. You cannot change the entire way you do your job to pacify one employee.

## MISTAKE #192
### An Employee Has a Complaint; I Did Something Wrong

The person may just be looking for attention and they think complaining will help; I consider that to be negative attention. There are people who need any attention; keep this in mind and try to determine if that is the situation.

Here are some tips to help you deal with chronic complainers:

- Whenever chronic complainers come to you with a problem, assign them a task. Do this each time they approach you with a complaint, and they will soon decide if the complaint is valid enough to bring to your attention.

- Do you have an employee who is a good listener? Can you assign the listener and the complainer to work together?

- Have you thought about installing a complaint box in the department? Tell team members that they need to submit their complaints on paper. If you get a lot of ridiculous complaints, you could review the complaints at your weekly staff meetings. Hopefully this will make the chronic complainers who harp on frivolous things to use better judgment before submitting future complaints.

> ## MISTAKE #193
> ### Complaints Are Taking Up Too Much of My Time
>
> One way to resolve this is to install a complaint or suggestion box. This will keep people from interrupting your day and will still guarantee you will consider them.

After a short time, the complainer should decide it is easier to bother someone else. But remember that even chronic complainers have a point sometimes. Listen to what they have to say before you dismiss it.

## CREATING A TEAM MENTALITY

Your department employees will work better as a team. There are many ways you can create the team mentality. We'll discuss various techniques and you can evaluate which will work for you.

The manager needs to convey the mission and goals for the team. This gives direction and purpose to the group. Your team needs to understand what you expect from them. Do they understand your goals? Explain the role each person plays in reaching them. Everyone needs to work toward these goals.

Teamwork is about working together. Do you discuss details with your team or do you just issue assignments? Effective communication is mandatory. The team needs to understand what they need to do and why. One way to ensure good

> ## MISTAKE #194
> ### I'll Tell My Team We Have Goals; That's Enough
>
> Be clear and specific with your team. They need direction, goals, and a mission. You can provide all those things. It makes a difference in how effective they become.

communication is to conduct consistent and effective meetings. These can be short and to the point; they don't have to be long and drawn out. Let your team discuss any thoughts and concerns during these meetings. Make sure they know their input is important to the team.

Remember that an effective and well-developed team doesn't take shape overnight. There will be challenges, and it takes time and effort. The effort will be worth your time in the end. A well-functioning team is invaluable to a manager.

When you begin, tell your team clearly and concisely what your plan is for your team. Make the plan and goals easy to understand. You need to accomplish whatever projects are assigned to you. With each new task, develop a plan. This becomes easier as you get more familiar with your employees and their skills. Use these abilities in the best way to accomplish the tasks.

Your team members need to feel important and needed. Ask for their thoughts and ideas at the start of each project. Their suggestions can help you to form a plan for the task. Participation helps your team members feel involved. They want to see it through to the end and have a stake in seeing it completed.

## MISTAKE #195
### I'll Outline the Plan; I Don't Need Input from My Team

Never underestimate how your team members can contribute. When you plan a project and as the plans progress, your employees can give you great insight. They approach the task from another angle and can offer valuable suggestions. Keep an open mind and hear what they have to say.

As you begin creating a team mentality, the changes you'll notice will be subtle at first. Don't be worried when you don't see sweeping changes right away. Any lasting and effective change takes time. You will see small changes as time progress. Help the team members with little things. Congratulate them on their successes and offer suggestions to improve when they experience failures.

---

### MISTAKE #196
#### I've Implemented the Plans and Will See Immediate Changes

It is wonderful to make changes and teach your employees to be more effective. Remember that the changes will be subtle. Don't expect big changes immediately, because you will be disappointed.

---

Finally, you need to be realistic about what you can accomplish and how long it will take. It won't happen overnight, but if you persevere, you will get results. Your efforts will build respect, trust, and confidence in your team. This will be invaluable to you and your team members.

Make an investment in your team. I'm not talking about a financial investment; this is an investment of your time and effort. You can invest this time in team meetings, classes, face-to-face meetings, and other similar activities. All of these things help you get to know them better and to find effective ways to motivate your team members.

## MISTAKE # 197
### I Shouldn't Have to Dedicate So Much Time to My Team

You can work this a couple of different ways. However, the most effective is to spend the extra time, find good people, and then train your team. If you build a lasting and strong team, that will make your job as a manager easier. They will know what you need and how you want things to be done. You shouldn't underestimate the long-term benefits of a well-trained team.

This will also help you build a productive and effective plan. Work with your team members and adjust your approach to suit the project and your employees. Your team needs to feel like they are a part of the task. This will help them take the project seriously.

## MISTAKE #198
### I Have a Management Style and My Team Must Adapt to That

There will be some concessions by your team, but you will also need to make some changes. People respond in different ways; an effective manager learns what style their team members respond to better. Some people need to be nurtured, others need direction.

Ensure that your team has the knowledge, skills, and information they need to do the job. They may need to be trained to use this knowledge in a productive way that will help the team. Once you train and motivate them, you need to ensure they have the right attitude. Each of these elements makes up the framework for your team.

An effective team displays the following characteristics within the team and when dealing with others. They operate as a unit and complement each other.

### Signs of a Well-Trained Team

- Understand goals

- Maintain quality

- Communicate and lead

- Offer support

- Clear instruction

- Results-driven

Your team may rebel since you are asking more of them than usual. It is good to have high expectations, and we've already discussed supplying the resources to help your employees reach these goals. When you properly train your team, they can then help you train any new employees that join your team.

## MISTAKE #199
### The Last Manager Didn't Expect Much, and I Shouldn't Either

The manager who doesn't expect much from his or her team is actually doing the employees a disservice. Most people respond well when they are pushed (in a tactful and effective way) to do more. This doesn't mean you should be unreasonable, but you should challenge your team members. Doing this successfully will make you all look good and you will grow.

Most businesses and managers do not fully utilize the abilities of their employees. This will give you an advantage over your competitors and should build loyalty within your team. People are more apt to stay in a job when they belong and feel they can contribute. You will be building these feelings and a great work attitude by systematically building your team.

When I managed a furniture store, we had complaints from our delivery drivers. They would complain there were too many deliveries, not enough time between these deliveries, and similar complaints. I sat down with them to explain things they could do to make the schedule work. These things included loading the truck in the order of the deliveries so they could take items off in order. When deliveries are organized by location, this saves a lot of time and gas, but sometimes the employees don't understand how that works for them. If they take a lunch break along the delivery route, this also makes the schedule work better for them.

Richard Henkel, Manager

# PART FOUR

# Dealing with Your Employees

Managers need an effective way to evaluate their employees' performance. This is why most businesses do periodic performance evaluations. Different businesses use different methods to evaluate their employees, and managers need to know how to create an evaluation form, how to review it with their team members, and what to do when their employees disagree with them.

# CHAPTER 13

# Evaluations

E ffective evaluations will help your team members grow. They also give you a chance to address problems with their behavior or performance throughout the year. Hopefully, you have been taking notes about employee issues when they're fresh in your mind. This is the time when you need those notes.

## MISTAKE #200

### *I've Held My Tongue About Their Performance; I Should Probably Keep My Concerns to Myself*

You should have already gone to the employee with any real and significant concerns. However, a performance evaluation is a written record of how employees do their jobs. Problems with an employee need to be mentioned, and employees should receive realistic ratings based on their performance.

I like to create employee files. They are a good place to keep notes about their performance. These files should be left in the office, but use a locked drawer. Personnel files should not be shared with anyone besides your boss. These are a place for you to keep confidential notes and details about the employee.

## MISTAKE #201
### I Can't Find Time to File Notes, So I Will Leave Them on My Desk Until I Have Time

Notes and comments about your employees should remain private. It's amazing how things can be misconstrued when others read your brief notes. Stick these in your pocket or under something in a drawer temporarily, but do not leave them lying on your desk.

When you have a large number of employees, keeping notes is especially important. With everything else you need to remember, it's easier to keep notes for the employee evaluations.

You also need to know that performance evaluations aren't the answer to all your problems. They are a great way to review the positives and negatives of the last year and to have time to focus on team members in more depth than usual. What if you tried to find solutions to some issues in the past and the employee didn't respond? You should mention those problems again, but that doesn't mean they will suddenly improve.

## MISTAKE #202
### Margaret Has Been a Problem, but That Will End with Her Evaluation

That might happen, but don't count on one evaluation to solve all your problems with any employee. You need to deal with problems throughout the year, and the employee's reactions to your assistance will be noted on that evaluation. Don't expect this one meeting to solve all employee problems.

In the past, I have given instructions and assistance to employees to resolve ongoing problems. If necessary, I would give them deadlines, which would coincide with the annual evaluations, to resolve the situation. In the extreme cases, I've said that we would review the status of their employment during the evaluation. This was a last resort, but also gave difficult employees a time frame to improve their attitude, behavior, or performance.

## MISTAKE #203
### It Should Be Enough to Tell Them Employees What They Need to Do

That is a good start, but the most effective way is to offer help and suggestions to make the needed changes and improvements.

You should be given instructions on how the company wants you to fill out evaluation forms, or your boss may work on the first one with you. Your boss or the human resources person should also give you a list of when each evaluation should be done. Some companies handle all evaluations at one time, while others are done on the anniversaries of employees' hire dates.

## MISTAKE #204
### I Guess I'm On My Own to Fill Out the Evaluation

Your boss should help you with the first couple of evaluations. The company may also have details on how they want you to complete the evaluation. If the business has a human resource department, you can also ask them for help.

Most evaluations have a list of statements, and you need to rate employees on these factors. You'll usually give employees a score from 1 to 5, with one being the lowest and 5 being the highest. You need to determine the rating for each element of the evaluation and then total them. This is usually used to determine what kind of raise the person will get that year.

> ## *MISTAKE #205*
> ### *I Could Invent My Own Scoring System*
>
> The ratings listed below are standard, and most people are familiar with them. Remember that the evaluation forms will go in employees' personnel files and other people will use them, so it's best to use a familiar system that others will understand.

Many forms use these standards for rating employee performance:

1. Unacceptable—Fails to perform the job. Below normal performance. Immediate improvement is needed to maintain employment.

2. Needs Improvement—Occasionally fails to perform the job. Performance must improve to meet job expectations.

3. Meets Expectations—Performs 100 percent of job duties in a satisfactory manner. Some supervision and guidance is needed.

4. Exceeds Expectations—Frequently exceeds job requirements. Objectives were accomplished above established standards.

5. Superior—Consistently works at above average level and exceeds employer expectations.

## CREATING EFFECTIVE EVALUATIONS

There are many aspects to a job; your evaluation needs to delve into these aspects. Many companies have developed evaluation forms that their managers use. Whether you use standard forms or make your own, determine what you need to accomplish before you start the evaluation process.

- Do you need to praise the employee?

- Are there problems that need to be handled?

- Are there things that were done well that you should mention?

- Do you need to let them know what was wrong and why it was wrong?

- Explain what they need to change about their performance.

- Decide how the employee can make the needed changes.

## MISTAKE #206
### I Could Focus on Basic Things Like Attendance and Attitude

To be more effective, you need to focus on a wide variety of skills and abilities. Great evaluation forms have various elements that paint a broader picture of an employee's performance.

What if you work for a company that doesn't have evaluation forms? You could approach your boss and ask if you can develop your own form to evaluate your team members.

## MISTAKE #207
### This Sounds Good, but My Company Doesn't Do Evaluations

You could speak to your boss about whether you could do evaluations in your department. It shows initiative and will help you analyze the performance of your employees and the entire team.

These are some items that will be on most evaluations. You will see a variety of these on different evaluation forms. It is also a good list to figure out what to cover on a personalized evaluation form. The items include the following:

- Adaptability
- Administration (if applicable)
- Attendance
- Attitude
- Behavior
- Communication
- Complete Work
- Cooperation
- Delegation (if applicable)
- Dependability
- Enthusiasm
- Initiative
- Interpersonal Skills
- Judgment
- Knowledge, Skills, and Abilities

- Leadership
- Maintaining Expenses
- Maintaining Inventory
- Meeting Quotas
- Meeting Attendance
- Meeting Deadlines
- Planning and Organization
- Promptness
- Punctuality
- Quality of Work
- Scheduling Ability
- Sticking to a Schedule
- Technical Skills
- Training Attendance
- Work Habits

## MISTAKE #208
### I Can't Believe That I Have to Evaluate an Employee on All Those Things

You don't need to rate employees on each of these things. This is a list of possible subjects to evaluate their performance. There are more, but you can choose the subjects that you are the most concerned about.

The aforementioned things are pretty standard. If you have the chance to personalize your evaluation, you would include skills and tasks that are important within your department or business. Those will vary greatly based on what your team members are required to do. Think of the tasks they do and what abilities are needed. You will want to add these items to the list if possible.

The more thorough the evaluation form, the more effective the review will be for the employees. This isn't just an idea to create more work; it can be very beneficial when it includes the skills your employees need and is handled properly. The information in the remainder of the chapter will help you make more effective evaluations.

## Conducting Evaluations

You should remind employees a week or two before you plan to meet for their evaluations. Set a time and meet in your office or another private place when the day arrives. At this point, you have filled out an evaluation for each employee, and you are ready to meet with each of them.

Since you are new to the job, it might be good to look over old evaluations to get an idea of employees' past performances. But do not fill out your evaluations based on the old scores unless your boss instructs you to do that. In that case, you should note that beside your signature and write how many months you worked with the employees. You can also see if the previous manager kept notes about the employees. These are only that person's opinions, but they could give you some additional insight.

### MISTAKE #209
*I've Only Been Here for a Few Months; I Can't Evaluate the Employees*

It is easier to do a thorough evaluation when you know the team members better, but you can gain additional information by talking with your boss or checking old evaluations.

After you conduct the evaluations and tally the scores, each employee should fall into one of these three categories:

1. Above Average—An above-average evaluation usually means a good pay raise and recognition for outstanding work.

2. Average—Most employees will fall into this category. You will still need to rate each point, but there probably won't be too much that is really good or bad. Employees may feel they are above average, but your results will show the specific areas where they need to improve.

3. Below Average—All employees will complain if they fall into this category. Even the employees who know they deserve the rating will want to argue with you. No one wants a low score in his or her file, and evaluation forms are always added to official employee files. Again, you will have the individual ratings to support the score that they received.

If you total the ratings and the scores seem wrong, review the evaluations again to be sure that you agree with the results. You need to stand behind your evaluations, so be sure of them before you meet with your boss and the employees.

## MISTAKE #210
### The Rating Total Doesn't Seem Right, but It Must Be Right

It's good to double-check your results since you will need to be sure about them. If an employee or your boss questions your results, you will need to explain your ratings. Make sure that they're right.

Sometimes evaluations need to contain specific goals for the following year. These could be based on changes within the department or things that you know employees are lacking. There needs to be logic to your conclusions and the recommendations that you make.

## MISTAKE #211
### I Would Like to Find a Way to Set Goals for Some Employees

Their evaluation is the perfect time to set and review goals. After you discuss the areas that need improvement, you can develop plans with your employees to help them improve and meet these goals.

During your meetings with employees, explain any high or low scores. The high scores will include praise for a job that was done well. In turn, the low scores will reflect on problem areas.

## MISTAKE #212
### I Can Try to Skip Over the Low Scores

You need to explain any high or low scores. The high scores give you a chance to praise employees, while the low scores are a chance to be specific about problems.

If you have discussed problem areas with an employee before, that also needs to be included and noted on the evaluation and discussed with the employee. You need to determine if there is a reason why the employee is not rectifying these problems.

## MISTAKE #213
### We've Discussed the Problems Before and It Didn't Help

When you discussed problems before, did you document them? You need to have documentation so that you can support any disciplinary action that is needed.

When you finish the evaluations with your employees, you need to let them review it and add their comments. Then they need to sign the forms.

## MISTAKE #214
### I'll Send the Evaluation to Human Resources without Our Signatures

You and the employee both need to sign the evaluation when you are finished. You need to include your comments about the evaluation and so does the employee.

There are managers who aren't comfortable giving evaluations, but they are an important part of the management process. They will help you monitor many different facets of your employees' performance.

## MISTAKE #215
### I'll Skip Evaluations Because They Make Me Uncomfortable

The first few evaluations are difficult, but they are important for your team and really need to be done. They will help you analyze all aspects of your employees' performance.

Employee reviews will help you gauge problems and trends within your department or business. The list puts the details in front of you and will help you monitor how the team is doing. This helps you detail a plan of action to improve your team and individual weaknesses. As you review evaluations with specific employees, there are some key points to convey:

- How are they doing?
- What should they do differently?
- What are their strengths?

- What are their weaknesses?

- How can they improve?

- What help do they need to excel?

- What can you do to help them?

## MISTAKE #216
### Evaluations Only Apply to Individual Employees, so They Can't Help My Whole Team

When you do employee evaluations, you can track changes and problems within your department. If many of your team members have the same problem, that could indicate they need more training or supervision in a certain area.

Part of your job is to help team members understand how they fit into the "big picture." This helps to create the team atmosphere. Help them to understand how they fit in and why their performance is important. Each person in the department or business has a specific role and needs to understand his or her part. A great time to discuss this is during evaluations.

## MISTAKE #217
### I Need to Evaluate Each Employee Individually

That is partially true, but you also need to see how the team members fit together and help them understand how they fit into the "big picture" for the company.

An evaluation is not just a once-per-year meeting with your employees. You need to do some parts of this work during the year. Keep track of the positive and negative things that employees do. Deal with issues as they arise, and don't wait until the evaluation to mention problems. The evaluation is a great time to review these details with the employee.

## MISTAKE #218
### I'll Wait Until the Review Before I Discuss Problems

That will not be as effective. It works better to discuss the problems throughout the year. You can then take action during the evaluation. When you leave a problem for a long time, it will get worse. It is good to take steps to resolve issues as they arise.

When you discuss your evaluation with an employee, be clear about what the employee did and did not do well. Be specific and give examples. Once you have explained the details, encourage conversation with the employee. This gives you the chance to see how they feel about what you said. It also gives them the chance to react and explain why they disagree or agree with your thoughts.

## MISTAKE #219
### Employees Get to Write Comments; Why Do They Need to Discuss It?

It's good to encourage your employees to discuss their evaluations. This gives you a sense of what they think and whether they are likely to make any changes. This is especially critical when there are problem areas.

It can be difficult to explain to employees what will happen if their performance doesn't improve. If you have tried to work with an employee repeatedly without improvement, you may need to discuss further action. This could include putting the employee on probation for a limited time. With ongoing performance issues, you need to take a firm stand, especially when you have discussed problems and the employee has not made the needed changes and improvements.

### MISTAKE #220
### I've Tried to Help Him Improve, But He Ignores Me; an Evaluation Won't Help

If you have tried to help an employee improve, you need to compile your documentation. When you write the evaluation, include all the things you tried and how they worked. In the evaluation you will review these facts with the employee. Then you can notify the employee about what will happen if things don't improve.

Let the employee know what they did well. Is there a way to use his or her past successes to improve their current performance? The employee may have the skills that are needed but isn't sure how to use them on a different task. This can be a great opportunity for you to help an employee improve.

### MISTAKE #221
### I'll Only Focus on the Bad Things

You need to talk about the positive things that happened during the year. The negatives are more complicated and need more explanation, but don't ignore anything that was positive.

Once you discuss the situation, it is good to develop a plan to help the employee reach the goals you discussed. It doesn't help to tell an employee to improve without giving him or her the tools to make it happen. You don't need to be elaborate or very detailed. You can list some specific things that you talked about in the evaluation that will help the employee.

## MISTAKE #222
### I Talked About All the Points on the Evaluation and Pointed Out the Problems; I'm Finished

After you explain the problems, you need to discuss a plan to help the employee improve. If he or she decides not to make improvements, then you can deal with it, but first allow a real chance to make the necessary changes.

After the evaluation, you need to follow up with your team member. This is especially critical when you put an employee on probation. Any evaluation and plan to improve needs follow up. There is no sense in going to all that trouble just to leave the employee dangling. When do your progress check, you can offer suggestions and praise.

## MISTAKE #223
### I Developed a Plan to Help the Employee; Now I'm Done

You are almost finished. After you develop a plan, you need to follow up with the employee. This will help you ensure he or she is making improvements and give you a chance to help the employee implement the plan.

## WHEN WORKERS DISAGREE WITH YOUR EVALUATIONS

Be aware that employees don't always agree with your evaluation of their performance. I've conducted many evaluations, and employees don't usually walk in and tell me all the mistakes they made over the last year.

Workers usually feel that you should have given them higher

marks. We all have opinions about how much we are worth and how good we are. This situation is no different. Some employees will use the fact that you are new against you. They might say they deserve higher ratings, but you don't know them well enough to give them the right evaluation. If this happens, you should discuss the situation with your boss.

---

### MISTAKE #224
#### I Hope the Employees Will Agree with My Evaluations

Be prepared that employees don't usually agree with negative evaluations. Many people think they deserve a better rating. Don't let that influence your rating. This is another reason why you need to be sure about your evaluation.

---

You may get a feeling that some employees are going to complain about their evaluation. I used to review the evaluation with my boss before I met with the employee. I always did this if it was going to be a low score, because I knew that the employee would complain.

---

### MISTAKE #225
#### Dwayne Will Be Mad About His Evaluation, but There's Nothing I Can Do

When you know someone is going to complain, you need to prepare for possible problems. You might want to talk with your boss before you meet with your employee. This works very well when the employee wants to complain and your boss already has the details.

---

Don't take up a lot of your boss's time, but you could make a copy of the evaluation for your boss and review the areas you are concerned about. When the employee is unhappy with your evaluation, he or she will complain to your boss. If you handle it this way, your boss is ready for the complaint, or you can tell the employee that you already reviewed it with your boss. I usually had my supervisor initial that they agreed with my conclusions. This defused situations before they could escalate. Before you involve your boss, however, make certain that your evaluation is fair and not clouded by your personal opinions.

## MISTAKE #226
### I Can't Think of Any Way That Employee Evaluations Will Impact Me Personally

You will have to deal with the employees after the evaluations are done and follow up on the plans you developed for them. When it is time for your evaluation, your boss will review how you handled your employees and it will affect your ratings.

Remember that part of your evaluation will be about your evaluation skills. When evaluations are handled well, they are very beneficial to you and the business. They will also become easier with practice. The first few evaluations may be difficult, but your boss can help you with those.

# CHAPTER 14

# Discipline and Firing

**T**here will be times when every manager needs to discipline employees. The way you deliver criticism and discipline makes a huge difference in whether it will be accepted and whether the employee will improve.

## MISTAKE #227
### *Ken Has Been a Nightmare to Deal with; He Needs to Know I've Had Enough*

I've had employees like that. You want nothing more than to tell them how much they irritate you and what a problem they are, but you cannot lose your temper or lash out at them.

These are some basic keys to effective discipline:

- Be encouraging

- Show perseverance

> ## MISTAKE #228
> ### I've Talked in Circles with Sarah Over the Last Two Weeks; That's Enough
>
> You need to talk with the employee, formulate a plan to help her improve, and spend some time trying to make it work. This will take longer than two weeks.

- Be realistic

- Remain tolerant

> ## MISTAKE #229
> ### Henry Has Been a Big Problem and I Can't Deal with Him Any Longer
>
> You probably don't have a choice. Again, you need to work with Henry to help him improve. When you move to take disciplinary action, be sure that you handled everything right. Then you can move forward with further action.

Let's discuss some techniques that will help you handle discipline effectively and in the right manner.

## USING DISCIPLINE WITH YOUR EMPLOYEES

These are three types of disciplinary action:

1. Verbal warning

2. Written warning

3. Termination

## MISTAKE #230
### I Want to Skip the Warnings and Terminate Jeff Today

That attitude and action can cause you and the company a lot of problems. The only time you can skip these steps is when the employee stole something or assaulted another employee. In any other case, you need to follow the policies that were established by the company.

You must follow the company procedures carefully and completely. Before you meet with the employee, plan what you will say. It is always helpful to make notes or an outline of the key things you want to say.

## MISTAKE #231
### I Know This Situation and Don't Need Notes; I Can Handle This off the Top of My Head

You probably feel that is true. The problem is that it's easy to lose your train of thought when you are in a stressful or high-pressure situation. Disciplining an employee is stressful. It's best to make some notes that you can refer to during your meeting.

When you are faced with a disciplinary situation, contact the human resources department. The people in human resources can give you information on the company policies to handle discipline issues. They may have written instructions, forms to complete, and so on. Or they may simply give you tips on how to handle the situation and what to avoid.

## MISTAKE #232
### Reprimanding Someone Can't Be That Involved; I'll Figure It Out

Most companies have specific policies about how to discipline employees. As a manager for the company, you need to follow these policies. The human resources department can be very helpful in discipline situations.

What if your company doesn't have a human resources department? Your boss or the owner would be the person to approach. He or she can tell you how it should be handled. Discipline is complicated and requires a delicate touch, so follow your boss's instructions.

## MISTAKE #233
### I Manage a Small Company That Doesn't Have a Human Resources Department, so I'll Just Wing It

In this case, you need to speak to your supervisor or the owner. He or she should have recommendations about how to handle employee discipline. You may be able to offer suggestions, but you need to follow your boss's directions.

Keep in mind that discipline is meted out to help the employee improve. It should never be used to punish an employee. When you have tried to work with the employee and you aren't making progress, you need to take disciplinary action. In extreme situations, you need to terminate an employee who doesn't improve, but we will discuss that at the end of the chapter. Before you terminate someone, though, try other avenues.

### MISTAKE #234
#### Jeremy Drives Me up the Wall; I'll Discipline Him and Show Him Who's the Boss

This may be tempting with some employees, but you cannot behave that way. It is unprofessional and can cause you future problems with the company. The employee could pursue legal action in extreme situations.

It's critical to document any disciplinary action that is taken. This begins when a problem first arises and you sit down with the employee to discuss it. You need to document what was said, the employee's reaction, any recommendation you made for the employee, and the date. These details will be invaluable if the situation doesn't improve. As I mentioned in the last chapter, you will also need this information for their evaluation.

When a disciplinary situation arises, what steps should you take? You need to talk with the employee in private. It might even be good to leave the department or your office. This will give you an uninterrupted chance to discuss the details. Tell the employee what is wrong and get his or her feedback. You shouldn't be surprised if they don't agree with your evaluation of the problem.

There are many different reasons why an employee might not be performing as well as he or she could. Listen to the employee and try to figure out what is going wrong. Some common reasons why employees have trouble include the following:

- Something or someone could be causing the employee to have difficulties. If the problem is at home, there is little you can do. However, if the problem is within your work area, you need to research the employee's claims. If you find that the employee has a valid problem, then that situation needs to be resolved.

- Does the employee need additional training to do the job better? This is something that you should check. Are there any classes offered that would be helpful? Is there another employee with the experience to train this person? When you decide to try this approach, keep an eye on the employee. Is he or she making a real effort to improve or is this a way to get out of work?

## MISTAKE #235
### Hal Told Me That He Doesn't Have the Training to Do the Job, but I Don't Believe Him

Even if you disagree, you still need to research the employee's claims. There could be a situation that is causing the problems. Try to keep an open mind and look into the potential problem. You will need to be able to prove that you evaluated the situation before you moved ahead with disciplinary action.

- The employee may try to blame someone else. It is easier to point the finger than to take responsibility for problems. You need to check the allegations, but be reasonable in your determination. Just because the employee blames someone, that doesn't mean it's a fact.

- Proceed carefully. Document what the employee says to you and verify whether the comments are true or false. You need to check and double-check your facts. Dealing with an unproductive employee every day is an ongoing hassle that needs to be resolved.

After you've taken the time to speak with the employee and hear his or her thoughts, researched each possibility, and checked to see if the complaints were valid, you can determine if the employee is the problem and if further disciplinary action needs to be taken.

Once you have researched to the employee's comments, you need to call another meeting. Let the employee know you researched each comment, and give a summary of what you discovered. If you found that the claim had no basis, you still need to be tactful and careful with your comments. You may be tempted to say many other things, but think before you speak and keep the exchange professional.

## MISTAKE #236
### I Researched Sandra's Claims and Found She Was Lying to Me; Now I Can Fire Her

You need to call Sandra in for a meeting and calmly discuss the situation. At this point, you need to issue a verbal or written warning, depending on what you have already done. Remain calm and professional, but be sure she knows you checked her claims, and tell her what you found.

When you disprove an employee's accusations, it is important to tell him or her that you will not accept any excuses. If you continue to accept excuses and diversions, it will make you look weak and ineffective. Once the disciplinary process begins, you must stand firm. This shows the employee that you are serious.

## MISTAKE #237
### I've Heard Enough Lies and Won't I Listen to Anymore

This is basically a true statement, but that isn't the way to handle it. Your research proved there was no basis for the comments and now you need to tell the employee that you won't accept any more excuses. What happens next is up to the employee and how he or she responds.

Keep the meeting under control. Don't make it long and drawn out or give yourself or the employee time to say too much. You need to be concise and direct with your comments. The employee may try to get you off the subject, but keep the discussion focused.

## MISTAKE #238
### I'll Drag Out the Meeting so I Can Watch Him Squirm

I know how appealing that sounds, but you cannot do that. You are the manager and you have to remain professional. Another problem is that you are likely to say something that will cause a problem if you talk too long. Keep the meeting short and to the point. That is better for everyone.

You may need to remind the employee that you tried to offer advice and suggestions but he or she ignored you. Situations reach a point where you have to take more serious action. This is when you need to bring in your boss.

## MISTAKE #239
### Monica Claims I Didn't Lift a Finger to Help Her

You know that isn't true. This is another time when you can pull your notes from her file and show her the documentation of your previous conversations. Your notes will show that you tried to help her on several occasions, and they should also show her reactions to your assistance.

## WHEN TO INVOLVE YOUR BOSS

Whenever there are serious employee issues, keep your boss informed. This is especially true when you have to take disciplinary action. You can meet with your boss and share the notes in the employee's file. This will bring your boss up to date and show that you have your documentation in order.

## MISTAKE #240
### I Can Handle Serious Discipline without Bothering My Boss

This is a time when you need to tell your boss about the situation. You can review your documentation with him or her, and this will help you both prepare for a meeting with the employee.

When problems arise while you are still new, it could be better for your boss to handle the discipline. This would be a great way for you to learn, especially if you sit in when he or she talks to the employee.

## MISTAKE #241
### I'm New, But Maybe I Can Muddle Through It

If you are very new, your boss or someone from human resources should handle the discipline. A new manager should learn by watching someone with more experience handle the actual meeting and discipline.

It's good to discuss other disciplinary actions with your boss. He or she may know of other things you can do to help resolve the problems. This is another time when your notes will be helpful to give your boss a complete picture of what you have tried.

## MISTAKE #242
### It's a Shame That We Can't Try Something Else to Help Kevin Improve

There could be something creative that your boss could suggest. This is another reason why it's good to talk with your boss or someone in human resources. They have more experience with these situations and could have some ideas that will resolve the problems.

Some businesses may go out of their way to avoid discipline. Other companies will enforce company policies more stringently.

You will learn more about how your company wants to handle employee problems. There are also many different ways to use discipline within the company. You should find that most managers develop their own styles, but keep your actions within the parameters for the company. Human resources can be a huge help in these situations.

There are some bosses who prefer not to be involved and may insist that you handle it personally. It is possible that your boss doesn't know how to handle the situation. In this case, your best course of action would be to talk with human resources. They know the regulations and can let you know how you should handle the problem.

When the situation escalates or the employee doesn't improve after repeated attempts to help, you need to consider terminating them.

## WHEN YOU NEED TO FIRE SOMEONE

Understand that there will be times when you cannot help an employee. Some people are unwilling to make the needed changes, and that is not a reflection on you. You need to know that some employees will make changes and others will ignore your attempts to help. You have done everything that is required of you and must move to more definitive action.

### MISTAKE #243
#### I Must have Failed Jerome; He Isn't Getting Better

Managers need to learn that they can't help everyone. An employee must want to improve and be receptive when you offer help. There's nothing you can do if an employee won't accept your help.

Your only option is to terminate the employee who cannot or

will not perform. When you get to that point, you need to move forward. Even though it's difficult, the existing situation is hard for you, other employees, and office morale.

> ## MISTAKE #244
> ### I Feel Like Lee Will Improve,
> ### so I Will Wait to Talk to Him
>
> That sounds like it should work, but when you delay in reprimanding an employee, you make a frustrating situation for yourself and your other employees. If the situation is serious, you risk harming the morale of the department or business.

Gather all your documentation and notify the employee that you need to meet. It would be good to have your boss attend. Update him or her before the meeting so you can present a united front to the employee. If your boss cannot or will not attend, have the meeting with someone from human resources.

It's good to hold this meeting away from your office for the following reasons:

- The employee could be emotional or want to argue.

- The meeting could get out of hand. If you expect that, you should have security or someone else close by to oversee the situation. This won't be necessary in most cases, but you know the employee and need to make this decision.

- If problems arise, you can leave and go back to your work area. Don't just walk out, but your boss or the person from human resources may indicate that you can leave.

Prepare for the employee's reaction. After several meetings with this person, you know how they will respond. Don't overreact and don't underestimate him or her.

Theft and physical assaults are situations that must be handled immediately. Almost every time, these problems will result in employee termination. It is critical to have someone dependable interview everyone that has information about the problem. This information should be gathered the same day while the memories are fresh. You should have the employees sign the notes about their recollection of events. Terminations because of theft or assault are likely to prompt court situations, so you need to have your documents in order.

## MISTAKE #245
### One of My Employees Assaulted Another Employee; I'll Throw Him Out

You should get any employees together who have information about the assault; have their statements documented and signed. You might suspend the employee until you have more information. Once you have a clear picture of what happened, you should talk with your boss or human resources and take definitive action. There is almost no reason to keep the employee. Violence cannot be tolerated in the workplace. To protect yourself and the company, it's good to look into the incident to see what caused the assault. If you find the employee is guilty and there were no extenuating circumstances, he or she should be terminated.

It's not pleasant to terminate an employee, but you need to determine what is best for the business or department that you manage. You cannot risk morale or performance problems with your team because of one person that is a problem.

## HANDLING SEXUAL HARASSMENT CLAIMS

We've all heard stories about sexual harassment situations. Some people snicker when the subject is mentioned, while others become outraged. The government has various laws and statutes that pertain to sexual harassment and how allegations of harassment need to be treated. Managers need to avoid anything that could be misconstrued as harassment.

The way you handle these situations can depend on the size of the company where you work. Large corporations must handle sexual harassment charges in certain ways, while smaller companies have more flexibility. Even with that flexibility, allegations must be handled.

> ## MISTAKE #246
> ### June Said Someone Is Harassing Her; I Want to Ignore the Situation
>
> You really need to deal with the situation. Is there someone in the company who is assigned to handle these problems? If so, it can be turned over to that person. Whether you handle it personally or turn it over to someone else, be sure that it is handled promptly.

Title VII of the Civil Rights Act of 1964 pertains to sex discrimination and applies to all employers with fifteen or more employees. Situations that would be classified as sexual harassment include the following:

- Unwelcome sexual advances.

- Verbal or physical requests for sexual favors.

- Verbal or physical conduct that is of a sexual nature.

- Conduct that impairs a person's employment and ability to do his or her job.

- Conduct that promotes a hostile, offensive, or intimidating work situation.

Sexual harassment doesn't have to be a man harassing a

woman or involve people of different genders, it just has to be unwelcome. Any employee or customer can harass an employee. Many people don't realize that people can file a complaint if they are offended by the conduct even if they are not personally harassed.

## MISTAKE #247
### The Situation That Was Relayed to Me Is About a Woman Harassing Another Woman; That Isn't Harassment

This can be classified as harassment and needs to be investigated. Harassment can include either gender and can include people of the same sex. Harassment can take many forms.

### How to Handle Allegations

Once improper behavior is alleged, you must investigate the complaint. The severity of the harassment will determine what sort of action should be taken. Any allegation must be evaluated on a case-by-case basis. You cannot make blanket assumptions about the alleged victim or harasser.

## MISTAKE #248
### We Could Make This Easier and Just Terminate Anyone Who Is Accused of Harassment

That might make your current situation easier, but it is not fair. Allegations of harassment need to be evaluated. The punishment should also be appropriate for the situation. There isn't one type of discipline that would be fair for each and every instance.

The person who investigates the allegation will consider the circumstances surrounding the alleged incident along with the context and situations surrounding the event. These can help explain different perceptions of a situation. That doesn't mean it should be explained away, but in fairness to both people, evaluate everything surrounding the incident.

### Preventative Measures

Every company needs to take action before any complaints are filed. Does the company have a policy that clearly states sexual harassment will not be tolerated? If not, a policy needs to be compiled and distributed to all employees. Make it clear that no form of sexual harassment will be tolerated.

It's advisable to include in your policy a statement that people will not be fired for filing a complaint or bringing the problem to the attention of management; this is one reason why many people will keep the information to themselves. Shame is another reason why people keep quiet. When a complaint is filed, it needs to remain private and should only include the people who are directly involved.

Once the policy is established and circulated, the company needs to set up guidelines for complaints to be filed. A designated person needs to handle complaints in an unbiased and thorough manner. This person needs to ensure complaints are handled promptly.

---

### MISTAKE #249
#### We Have a Policy, but We Only Show It to Employees When There Are Problems

It's possible that making the company policy known will help eliminate potential problems. Make the employees know that the company will not tolerate sexual harassment.

---

Managers need to be given instruction on how to:

- Keep their eyes open for sexual harassment situations.

- Watch for potential harassment situations.

- Avoid behavior that could result in sexual harassment accusations.

The person who evaluates a harassment claim needs to review all evidence. Some people will volunteer to come forward and share what they know, but others may hesitate to share the details they have. All information is needed in order to take the appropriate action.

Each allegation needs to be reviewed thoroughly and with an open mind. If the allegations are substantiated, appropriate action must be taken. This could be a verbal reprimand or more severe action. Again, be sure the discipline is appropriate for the offense. If the inappropriate behavior persists, the employee may need to be terminated. As with other situations, document each step of the process for the employee files.

The situations in this chapter can be difficult, but they are all necessary parts of your job as a manager. Go to your boss or human resources for additional help on how to handle any situations that arise.

I often was the head of a hiring committee, replacing departed employees. Most of the time things went very well, but on one occasion I found myself the target of a discrimination case because the committee did not select a black woman with whom I worked. Luckily, I had kept very precise notes on the process, maintained ranking sheets, and was able to relate to the attorneys the discussion I had with the group prior to the interview, stressing that personalities or knowledge of the candidates had no part in the process. We were to ask all the exact questions and rank the candidates based on their answers. Because I was the one person who ranked her highest, it was hard for them to pinpoint that I had any bias. The lawsuit is still ongoing, but now she is just suing the employer. It's very important to keep documents about interviewing processes for quite a while after you hire someone.

Ginger Simpson, Author
**www.gingersimpson.com**

# CHAPTER 15

# Effective Meetings

At times, you will need to meet with your team members. This chapter includes tips to make your meetings more effective. Meetings can be a waste of time or beneficial for your team; how you handle meetings will make all the difference.

## CONDUCTING AN EFFECTIVE MEETING

Meetings with your team should be low stress and informal. This will allow you to practice conducting meetings with familiar people. Common meeting pitfalls are easy to avoid if you keep your eyes open.

## MISTAKE #250
### I Would Be Too Nervous Conducting a Meeting in Front of My Team

This may be true at first, but it becomes easier as you get to know your team members better. Keep in mind that this is good practice for a time when you need to need to conduct a meeting with other supervisors.

One of your first priorities is planning when to have meetings. You don't need to have a meeting just because someone suggests the idea. There should be a real reason for it. An unnecessary meeting can be a waste of time and will distract your employees.

## MISTAKE #251
### I Will Call a Meeting Each Morning

You probably don't need to have meetings every morning. You might want to post a simple sign on the time clock to notify your team members if there will be a meeting that morning. That would allow your team to get to work without coming to you for an unnecessary meeting.

There are some good reasons for a new manager to hold meetings:

- Meetings with your team are a good way to get to know them.

- It's a chance for you and the employees to vocalize ideas and thoughts.

- It's a good time to ask employees for their comments.

## MISTAKE #252
### I Should Insist My Employees Not Talk During Meetings so We Can Get to Work Sooner

You should encourage employees to speak up, even if it will make your meetings a little longer.

- You will become familiar with your employees in this setting.

- Are certain employees always quiet? Encourage them to join in the conversations.

- New managers might want to have regular meetings for the first month or two and then scale back the frequency once they are established.

## MISTAKE #253
### I Could Have a Meeting Every Morning for the First Year and Then Figure Out What to Do

It would be good to evaluate the need for meetings after a month or two. You could also reevaluate your schedule each month. There is no reason to have a meeting every day unless your team needs them and you can make them an effective use of your time.

- A quick meeting can be good. This gives you a way to pass out assignments and answer employee questions before the workday starts.

## MISTAKE #254
### We Could Have a Meeting Right After Lunch

This could be distracting for your team. A meeting first thing in the morning or last thing in the afternoon seems to work the best. These are the least disruptive times of the day. I like morning meetings because they help start your day with a focus.

When you schedule a meeting, it's good to make simple notes about the items you need to share with your team. This will help you stay focused. Try to keep your meetings around ten to fifteen minutes in length. This provides time to address the important topics without cutting into work time. Keep the meeting focused on the subjects you need to discuss.

## MISTAKE #255
### Someone Told Me an Effective Meeting Must Be at Least Thirty Minutes, but I Don't Know What to Talk About

You will be relieved to know that the most effective meetings are around ten to fifteen minutes. This gives you time to make announcements and answer some questions. There could be times when there is something more detailed to discuss, but this probably won't happen often.

Here are some common pitfalls that you may need to face:

- Some employees may want to give you a hard time.

- You may have one or two people who keep interrupting the meeting.

- Disagreements between employees can get out of control.

How should you deal with these problems? Let's look at them individually.

### Your Staff Is Giving You a Hard Time

Employees may voice personal complaints in the meeting. These complaints should be handled in private. There's no reason to waste the group's time. Handling these personal complaints in private can prevent any embarrassment for the team member.

> ## MISTAKE #256
> ### It Might Be Good to Stop the Meeting and Deal with Laura's Complaint
>
> This could be a personal complaint or an attempt to disrupt the meeting. It would be good to get more details and decide if Laura mentioned a group complaint or if it only bothers her. Personal complaints should be handled in private.

Do any other people join in with similar complaints? If so, talk to each person who has this complaint. Try to draw the employees into a simple conversation to see if others feel the same. When an employee wants to cause problems, they will bring an irrelevant complaint to you, so this probably won't be a group complaint.

The employees may complain about something you don't know anything about. In this case, you need to find out more details before you respond. It is critical that you don't make any statements or promises before you get more details.

### MISTAKE #257
### My Employees Put Me on the Spot
### and I Had to Answer Them

Effective managers never let their employees put them on the spot. If they try, tell them that you will look into it and get back to them. This approach gives you control of the situation. Be sure to follow-up or you will lose credibility.

It's important that you stop employees who try to distract the group and cause unnecessary problems for you. After a couple of unfounded complaints, call the employee into your office to discuss this behavior. It should be clear that others aren't joining in the complaints. Tell the employee that these are personal complaints and it is inappropriate to bring them up at a group meeting. If it continues, you may need to take more action.

### Maintain Control

At times you will have two or three people who will try to take over your meeting. You have to squelch their behavior. This doesn't help your team and it undermines your authority. You must tactfully stop these interruptions.

### MISTAKE #258
### I Cannot Maintain Order at the Meetings
### Because of a Few Disruptive People

You have to maintain control of your meetings. When you lose control, there is no reason to have a meeting. You don't accomplish anything positive when your employees take control.

You might notice that some of your team members are quiet and rarely participate. It's good to encourage them to enter the discussion. Many times, the best suggestions come from people who say very little.

### MISTAKE #259
### Its Nice When Some Employees Stay Quiet During My Meetings

Don't dismiss people because they are quiet. They could have great ideas but just need you to encourage them to speak up in the meetings.

## Disagreements Between Employees

Occasionally there will be disagreements between some employees. However, voicing those differences and disrupting your team meetings is not acceptable. When arguments start, you need to stop them. Get the employees to calm down and get the meeting back on track. If you feel like it's necessary, call the employees into your office for a private meeting later.

Is there a way to agree with both individuals? Sometimes you can say they are both right. You may need to look into the comments and then give your thoughts. Another idea is to ask them both to justify their viewpoints on paper. This is more difficult than spouting ideas in the middle of the meeting. If they aren't committed to their arguments, they won't want to take time to explain them on paper.

### MISTAKE #260
### Three Employees Argue at Each Meeting, but I Ignore Them

You can't ignore them. Call these employees into your office. Tell them to write a justification for their side of the argument. Let them know that they can't argue in a group meeting, but when their justifications are complete, you will meet with them. Chances are they won't want to go to the effort to write down the details. If they do, then have a brief meeting with them and let them voice their thoughts.

Each of these tips can help you learn to control your meetings and to make them more effective. You don't want to waste time with your employees. Make sure your meetings benefit your team instead of distracting from their jobs.

## PRODUCTIVE MEETINGS

Not only do you need to control your meetings, but you also need to make them productive. Sit down and think about business meetings that you attended. Do you remember what worked and what didn't? That's a good place to start. You know what you responded to at meetings. Now, how can you make your own meetings more productive for your employees?

One way to make your meetings more productive is to only have meetings when you need to convey information to your team. Do you have a meeting because it's on the schedule or because you have something to say? Any meeting you have needs to be important and necessary. If there is nothing important to convey, you need to cancel or postpone the meeting.

> ### MISTAKE #261
> ### The Last Manager Had a Meeting Every Monday; the Team Expects a Meeting
>
> Is there information that you need to share with your team? Do you want to make an announcement? Is there a valid reason to have the meeting? If not, then you should cancel and reschedule when you have a reason to meet.

Why interrupt your employees' work if it isn't necessary? Keep in mind that your employees aren't performing their job tasks while they are sitting in an unnecessary, unproductive meeting.

> ## MISTAKE #262
> ### I Don't Want Some Employees to Feel Left Out, so I'll Invite Everyone to the Meetings
>
> You are paying each of these people to attend the meeting. Only people who need to participate should attend.

Plan your meetings in advance. Make simple notes about any topics or announcements that need to be made. This will keep you on target and ensure you cover the important information. You can make this work by using time efficiently, encouraging communication, and making sure your meetings are productive.

> ## MISTAKE #263
> ### I'm Running Late for Work; I'll Have to Conduct the Meeting off the Top of My Head
>
> You shouldn't conduct a meeting without a plan or notes. It might be better to reschedule the meeting if you don't have a plan.

Whether your employees are working at their jobs or sitting in an unproductive meeting, they are being paid. How much does it cost you to have fifteen or twenty people sitting in an unnecessary meeting? It's only worth the payroll if the meeting is productive.

Ask yourself the following questions. They will help you compose a schedule and plan for your meeting:

- Do we need a meeting? Don't have a meeting just because of the day of the week. You have a lot of ways to communicate and disperse information. Do you need to have a meeting?

- Which employees need to attend? When your entire team comes to the meeting, who is answering the phones and helping customers? You must decide which people are needed.

- How long do I need for the meeting? The meeting should be as short as possible. Most meetings can be short and to the point. Planning what needs to be said will help you keep the meeting short.

- Does anyone else need to participate? If so, make a list and decide how much time they will have to talk. Set a time limit before the meeting starts and enforce it.

- What are my goals for the meeting? Make sure the purpose of the meeting is firm in your mind before it begins. This helps you stay focused. When others speak, it is good to let them know the goal for the meeting. Their segments should contribute to that goal.

Think about these specifics before you schedule a meeting. The answers to these questions will help you have productive meetings and will keep you from wasting payroll dollars on unnecessary meetings.

When you have important information for your employees, determine the best way to communicate this to your team. If a meeting is your best option, decide what you need to say, how long it will take, and which employees need to attend. All of these things will help you conduct productive and effective meetings.

The department director conducted meetings each day at 7 a.m. and 8 a.m. This allowed the nightshift and dayshift employees to attend one or the other. We covered any special announcements and gave out any unusual work assignments at this time. If there was no business, we could just wish the employees well and then get everyone to work. This also gave us a chance to be sure everyone got to work on time.

Anonymous

# CHAPTER 16

# Scheduling

There are many reasons to create an effective schedule for your team. In some companies, everyone works Monday through Friday during the day. It's easier to plan schedules in those environments, but different scheduling can present problems for new managers.

---

### MISTAKE #264
#### *We Work One Shift Monday through Friday; My Schedule Couldn't Be Complicated*

You are one of the fortunate managers who will have an easier time with your schedule. Don't relax too much, though, until you learn to work with vacation-day requests and employees who need time off.

---

For managers in situations with various shifts, it's a different scheduling situation. There could be day shifts, night shifts, evenings, weekends, and holidays. Each of these shifts has different needs and requirements, and most employees have conflicts with certain work hours.

In Chapter 10, I mentioned that you have to be honest about work hours when you interview prospective employees. If this is not handled in the beginning, you cause unnecessary hassles for yourself when you schedule team members for unpopular shifts.

## MISTAKE #265

### I Didn't Tell Maria That Employees Have to Work One Weekend a Month; I'll Deal with It When She's Scheduled

Maria will notice the weekend shifts on the schedule. To be fair to her, this needs to be mentioned during the interviewing process and certainly before she is hired.

There may be times when you have rush deadlines to meet or there is less work than usual. Each of these things can affect the number of man-hours you need. In other businesses, there is a demand for everyone to work at least forty hours each week. You will become familiar with the needs of your department or business.

In my experience, people who manage small businesses have more varied scheduling needs. In a departmental situation, the company usually dictates what is to be done and it is fairly routine. This chapter is directed toward small-business managers, but it also includes some tips for departmental managers.

## MISTAKE #266

### I Manage a Department in a Large Company; That Means I Won't Have Any Scheduling Issues

You will probably have fewer conflicts, but every manager has some issues to handle. There will be vacation days and possibly some overtime. You can find some tips in this chapter that will help you.

# KEEPING EMPLOYEES HAPPY WITH SCHEDULES

Keep employees happy with their schedules. That is harder than it sounds. Once you get employees into a scheduling groove, it is easier, but there may be certain shifts that no one wants to work. If you manage a business that is open nights, weekends, and

> ## MISTAKE #267
> ### I Told My Employees That Weekends Are Necessary; They Can't Complain About Them
>
> You made it clear what was needed, but they might still complain at times. If you can work around family and personal commitments, that would help morale, but don't let the employees dictate how you schedule.

holidays, someone must work those shifts.

Here is one scheduling scenario I worked with when I managed a pizza shop:

1. Inside shifts—Cooks and prep work.

2. Outside shifts—Drivers.

3. Morning and afternoon shifts—Short and long shifts.

4. Evening and night shifts—Short and long shifts until 2 or 3 a.m.

5. Most holidays and all weekends.

6. Most types of weather; closed for ice and snow when it got bad.

7. Super Bowl Sunday was mandatory for all employees— Several employees wanted off every Sunday for a day of worship.

8. College events when all employees had to work. This
   included my college students (who comprised 90 percent of
   the staff) who had to work during homecoming, exam week,
   etc.

When I interviewed potential employees, I was very clear about
the schedule we worked. There was no room to doubt what would
be expected of them, so I got few arguments. I'm sure this would
have been different if I had only skimmed over the hours they
would be expected to work, but I could make hiring decisions
based on their willingness to work the shifts I needed to fill.

## MISTAKE #268
### I Need Everyone for a Sale, but Some People Want to Be Off That Day to Attend Church

This sort of situation should be rare. For one week they should be able
to go to church in the morning and work that afternoon or evening.
Many people do that each weekend. I wouldn't schedule them during
church hours, but a different shift should be workable.

Some employees prefer day shifts while others prefer night shifts.
When you consider employees for nightshift work, remember
that there will be minimal supervision. This means they will have
to motivate themselves to get the work done. Not everyone can
do that, so you will need to keep an eye on their work and their
attitude.

## MISTAKE #269
### I Have an Employee Who Slacks If I Don't Watch Him; Now He Has Volunteered to Work Nights

Consider this carefully, and find ways to track the work that employees
like this do. People who work shifts with limited supervision need to
have initiative, otherwise you may be paying someone to sleep.

One place I worked, there was a nightshift person who restocked a critical area. He was hired to replace a woman who had done a great job. By the second week, his work started to suffer. A supervisor discovered that he rushed through his assignments and then curled up in the office to sleep for hours. One morning, the assistant director came in early to wake him up and fire him.

## MISTAKE #270
### This Scheduling Is Really Complicated; I Just Can't Get a Handle on It

You can make a chart that shows each shift you need to fill. This makes it easier to be sure you have enough people staffed and to track when each person is scheduled.

Sit down and look at the shifts you need to fill each week. When you first start working on a schedule, it can be helpful to make a chart with all the shifts for the week. This lets you insert employee names and see the entire week at once. Then you can keep a tally at the bottom of how many hours each person will work. It will also help to rotate who works weekends.

## MISTAKE #271
### I Can't Find an Easy Way to Rotate Who Works Which Weekend

The simplest system I've found is to work one weekend and be off the next. These employees would also have one day off during each week. This cuts your staff in half but alternates which weekends they work and keeps the business staffed without overtime concerns.

Improper scheduling can affect morale. Work within the employees' needs and desires when possible, but you do have to fill the work shifts. This is especially difficult during prime vacation times and around major holidays. I don't know of many businesses that have additional people on staff to fill in for these times. With budgeting restraints, it isn't feasible, so the effective manager may need to get creative in order to get the work done and keep the employees happy.

---

### MISTAKE #272
#### I'm Going Crazy Trying to Make Everyone Happy and Having Enough Staff for Our Shifts

You need to understand that there are times when you cannot make everyone happy. A top priority is to make sure you are staffed and the work gets done. As harsh as it sounds, pleasing everyone else is secondary.

---

Some managers feel that hiring many part-time people is the answer, but that can actually increase your headaches. I've always found it easier to juggle fewer people, especially since that means fewer people to satisfy.

---

### MISTAKE #273
#### I'll Just Hire Five Part-Time People and They Can Fill in the Problem Shifts

There can be several problems with this solution. Part-time staff may not be available when you need them. Another problem is that too many part-time people could impact the number of hours you have available for your full-time employees. One or two part-time people in a crunch can be good, but try not to rely on this solution too often.

---

Once you get a regular routine established, most employees will have similar schedules each week. This gives some consistency to their weeks and cuts down on employees who don't show up for their assigned shifts.

## MISTAKE #274

### My Boss Wants Me to Keep Our Man-Hours Low; Maybe I Could Schedule One Less Person per Shift

You can try this, but somehow you still need to get the work done. This can be rough and you have to be willing to work twice as hard. It's more productive to schedule the right number of people.

Some of these issues can be resolved if you find a few people who want extra shifts or an occasional shift. You usually need to schedule each person for less than forty hours per week. The people who are the most willing to work extra hours already have forty, but not always. Be very conscientious about your budget, and do not schedule more people than you need.

## MISTAKE #275

### I Need to Find a Way to Motivate My Team Members to Be Flexible for Me; I'm Not Sure How to Make That Work

It is a well-known fact that employees work harder and make concessions for a boss they like and respect.

You will discover that most people will be more flexible for a boss who treats them with respect.

## MISTAKE #276

### I Could Make a Few Exceptions for a Couple of Employees

It's better to stick to the rules you established. Your team needs consistency, and scheduling is a part of that. When you stand by the policies, it's less confusing. That makes it easier to get employees to follow the rules.

You can also save a lot of hassles if you set rules about taking time off and stick to them. The more consistent you are, the fewer problems you will have. Let your team members know what you expect, and don't deviate from that.

## ELIMINATING TARDINESS AND ABSENTEEISM

It's a hassle when your employees are tardy or absent. Both situations cause problems. With either of these problems, make a definite stand about it in the beginning. If employees sense you will let them get away with being late or absent, some will take advantage of you.

---

### MISTAKE #277
#### This Is Only the Third Time Roy Has Been Late; Maybe This Problem Will End Soon

When you let employees be tardy, the problem usually gets worse. Being tardy is distracting and cuts into their work time and performance.

---

You need to set a good example. Are you at work early or do you race in the door at the last minute? This sets a bad example. There will be occasions when you will be late, but it should be a rare occurrence.

## MISTAKE #278
### I Was Late a Few Times and Now My Team Members Are Coming in Late

Employees look for excuses to do things. When you set rules, you need to live up to them as well. You are the manager, and you need to do your best to lead by example. People follow an example better than they follow rules.

This is something that most managers have to deal with, and you need to know what the company expects. In order to enforce the rules, you need to know what they are and how the company handles them.

Did the previous manager enforce the rules about being tardy or absent? If not, this will make your job more difficult. One way to establish your ground rules is to call a meeting and make your stand clear. You might create a simple handout that outlines the policy on being tardy or absent. It could also include details on any disciplinary action that will be taken for consistent tardiness or absenteeism.

## MISTAKE #279
### The Last Manager Let Employees Arrive Late and Now They Won't Listen to Me

You need to make it clear that the previous manager isn't in charge. Make your policy clear from the beginning and stand by your decision. It's good to make the new policy clear at a meeting. That allows everyone to hear it at the same time and should cut down on confusion.

When you have enough information to establish your stand on these issues, there are several ways you can circulate the word to your team:

- Make an announcement in a meeting to let all employees know what the rules are and that they will be enforced.

- Make the details clear for your team. Explain what is expected and how exceptions and problems will be handled.

- Stand firm when someone is late. Show the team that you were serious and there will be repercussions for being late or absent.

- When an employee is repeatedly late or absent, you must take action. This shows the employee and other team members that you were serious and they need to be in attendance.

Like most things in management, the longer you wait to make your stand known, the harder it is to enforce the rules.

## MISTAKE #280
### I Don't Want to Seem Mean, so I'll Wait a Month or Two Before I Enforce the Rules

You should start off on the right foot. This includes enforcing the rules from the beginning. You set a bad precedent with your employees if you let the rules slide in the beginning.

There may be employees who call in sick or don't show up for work. Keep an eye on these situations. If one or two people get away with this, others will try it too.

> ## MISTAKE #281
> ### The Excuses Are Lame, but They Do Make Some Sense
>
> Employees will think of all kinds of interesting and entertaining excuses. That doesn't mean they are acceptable. You need to stand your ground and insist they follow the policies.

# HOW TO DENY REQUESTS FOR TIME OFF

At this point you have established that employees cannot be late or absent. Now you have to decide whether they can take time off. Each company has its own rules about vacation days. Take this into consideration when you discuss this with employees.

I kept a tabulation of vacation time with my copy of the schedule and updated it each week. The calendar with upcoming scheduled vacation time was also on that clipboard. This made it much easier to answer questions when team members approached me about time off.

Each employee has a limited number of days they can take off and be paid. When they are running out of vacation days, remind them about how many days they have per year. Once those days are gone, they will not be paid if they miss any more work.

We all want to help people who need a day off, but you also need to ensure that the work is done. When you are facing a deadline, there will be times when you cannot approve time off. This can be a tough situation to handle.

## MISTAKE #282
### I Want to Help, But I Can't Find a Way to Make It Work; I Must Be Doing Something Wrong

You probably aren't doing anything wrong. There will be times when you can't approve requests for time off. That is simply part of management.

Here are some common instances when employees need time off but situations make it difficult or impossible for you to grant their request:

- Deadlines looming—If you have critical deadlines to meet, you may have to suspend any days off until the deadline is met.

- Too many days off—When an employee requests a lot of days off, you may have to stop granting their requests.

- Too many employees are off—This can be a real issue at the height of vacation season and when people are out sick.

- They didn't handle the request in a timely manner—Did the employee have an appointment scheduled but they didn't tell you until a few days before?

- Employee has no more time—The employee might have used all their vacation days and you need to deny any further requests.

- Others already put in a request—If you have approved for others to take a certain day off, then you have to deny additional requests. There must be enough people on the schedule to get the work done.

Employees never like to hear "no," but at times, you don't have a choice. Your employees will learn their lessons and this will make future requests easier to handle.

# OVERTIME

Does your company accept overtime? This may seem like a funny question, but many companies will not allow it. It's an incredible expense to the employer, and very few projects justify that kind of added cost. You need to find out what the company policy is for overtime.

## MISTAKE #283
### If the Work Isn't Done, Then We Have to Work Overtime

When your department doesn't complete their projects and assignments, your boss will want to know why. Remember that overtime is very costly and your boss doesn't want to spend money for overtime very often. You may need to reorganize your employees or the way assignments are handled. There may be overtime occasionally, but it cannot be on a regular basis without your boss's approval.

Most employees will have issues about overtime. Some feel like forty hours is enough. Other employees understand they will be paid very well to work overtime and try to get extra hours whenever possible.

When overtime needs to be worked, ask who wants the additional hours. Keep in mind that employees who initially volunteer for overtime may not want to work overtime for long periods of time. Make sure your employees who show initiative aren't overworked.

## MISTAKE #284
### When I Need Overtime Workers, I Could Pick a Name from the Roster

It's better for morale to ask if anyone wants to work overtime. If this doesn't get any volunteers, you may have to draft people. It's good to give them the choice first in case anyone wants the additional hours.

If you are forced to make an overtime schedule, be fair with the assignments. Don't schedule the same people all the time, but do try to space these shifts out over time. It's also good to allow employees to switch shifts if they approve the changes with you. This will give the employees some flexibility and allows you to be sure some people don't get too much overtime.

## MISTAKE #285
### The Same People Always Volunteer; They Don't Seem Excited About the Additional Hours, but They Agree to Work

Are these the same people who always offer to do extra work? If so, try to find someone else. You don't want to risk overusing your key people.

You may notice that some employees work slowly during their regular shifts, making it mandatory that they work overtime to get their assignments done. You will learn how much work an employee should be able to do in an eight-hour day. There should be a good reason if they fall behind. An occasional day behind is understandable, but you must talk with them if it happens more often.

## MISTAKE #286
### There Are a Few People Who Need to Work Most Saturdays to Get Their Work Done

This is something you need to check into. Are these people working consistently during the week? It might be good to verify how productive they are Monday through Friday. Some employees have learned they can get overtime by doing less during the regular workweek. You cannot let them do this.

As soon as you know there will be overtime work, let your team members know. Don't spring it on them at the last minute. Try to be understanding with people who have real difficulties in their personal lives because of the overtime.

## MISTAKE #287
### The Parents in My Department have Difficulties Working Overtime, so I'll Make Overtime Mandatory for Single Employees

There are businesses that have this policy. They don't state that, but scheduling practices indicates that is the case. This is unfair to your single employees. There could be other factors that should be considered instead of just their marital status or whether employees have children.

Scheduling is tough, but with practice it gets easier. There are some companies where you will never have to write a schedule. In others, you will need to write schedules each week. Your boss or someone in human resources should be able to help you for the first few weeks.

Keep your employees' needs in mind, but you must have enough people to get the work done. It's good to give in to employee schedule requests when you can, but understand it won't always be possible. Set the guidelines for requesting time off and scheduling vacation and stand firm with your employees. They will learn how to handle requests, and your consistency makes it easier for everyone to get their jobs done.

# PART FIVE

# The "Big Three" Topics

*Communication, delegation, and motivation are the most critical elements of being a manager. If any of these three things are missing, it is extremely difficult to be an effective manager. All of the issues in this book are important and necessary, but you need to pay special attention to these three chapters.*

# Communication

Communication is the first of the "Big Three" topics that we'll address. Communicating effectively with your employees will make your business run more smoothly and help you work together more effectively as a team.

## MISTAKE #288
### I Can Talk to People; That's Enough

Actually, it's not enough. Communicating is more than just talking. It involves making sure that you listen as effectively as you speak, and that you express yourself clearly and positively. All good leaders and managers need to motivate their people, and effective communication is a great place to start.

## Communicate with Employees

The best time to establish communication with your employees is right from the beginning. Show your employees from the start that you will talk through situations and explain your reasoning with them. They need this from you and it helps establish a trusting and respectful relationship between you.

---

### MISTAKE #289
### There's a Lot to Do in the Beginning; I'll Talk with Them Later

You will never get another chance to make a good first impression, so you need to impress your team from the start. You don't need to learn everything about your employees, but take the time to learn their names. Another useful thing is to learn what they do in the business. Who can explain that better than the employee? That gives them a chance to tell you what their responsibilities are and it will show that you want to learn about them and their job.

---

How can you establish good communication from the beginning?

- Be straightforward and honest from the start.

- Don't avoid questions.

- Be patient and repeat answers if needed.

- Explain a new procedure more than once, especially if it is complicated.

- When something is wrong, talk through the problem and solution.

- Deal with problems when they happen. Don't ignore them.

- Correct employees immediately. Don't wait until later.

- Explain thoroughly when things need to be done another way.

- Ask for employee suggestions when discussing procedural changes.

- Be tactful when suggesting a different way to do things.

As a new manager, you will find that open and honest communication can make your job easier. In turn, holding back information or keeping things from your employees can make your job more difficult. There will be other difficulties, but good and effective communication can help you work out problems on the job.

---

### MISTAKE #290
### I Have a Job for Joe, but He Doesn't
### Need All the Details

It is much more efficient to give Joe all the details in the beginning. He will make decisions about the project based on the information you supply. If he is only working with limited information, he could easily make the wrong decisions. This will cause problems and delays in the project.

---

Keep in mind that employees might hold back and not work their hardest if they don't respect you. If you keep things from them unnecessarily or refuse to communicate with your team members, you might find that keeps them from having respect for you.

## MISTAKE #291
### I Don't Need Their Respect;
### They Just Need to Do Their Job

This is true, you don't need their respect to get any work out of them. But, if you want them to work hard for you, then you will need to earn their respect. Communicating effectively is one of the best and easiest ways to earn employees' respect. In turn, they will earn your respect by doing a superior job.

Many times, your employees won't work their hardest if they don't respect you. I can tell you from personal experience that employees work harder for a boss they trust and respect. If you want your team members to excel and take on added responsibility, they need to be able to talk with you.

Employees need to feel they can come to you with problems and issues on the job. What will happen when they have a problem with a project that needs your input and they don't come to you for help? You can save a lot of hassle if you keep the lines of communication open with your employees. Make sure they know they can approach you with problems and concerns.

## MISTAKE #292
### They Shouldn't Have to Bother
### Me with Every Problem

Who should your employees go to with their problems? You are their manager and you are the one who needs to answer their questions. It is also your job to help them feel comfortable bringing their problems to you. If they don't, then you may not know about problems until they are out of control. It is much better to encourage your employees to bring these problems to you early.

At times your employees will need additional direction or correction. You can prepare for this situation by finding time to talk with your employees and getting to know them. Don't spend hours talking about personal things, but get to know some more about them. This will make it easier to discuss the difficult situations that will arise in business.

Explain to your team members when they want something and you cannot make it happen. All employee requests are not possible. You need to understand these situations and deal with them effectively.

### MISTAKE #293
#### I Told the Team That It Can't Be Done; That's Enough

That would be easier for the moment, but your team members deserve an honest and complete answer. You need to explain why something can't be done. Employees will usually handle it fine when you take the time to explain why something isn't possible. Remember how you felt when your parents said "Because I said so."

When employees make requests that you cannot grant, you'll make your denial easier if you explain why what they are asking for is not possible. It's not effective to simply say "I said no" or "You can't do that because I say you can't." That will not work with employees. Give them the reasons. This shows that you respect them and have taken the time to help them understand.

## MISTAKE #294
### My Employees are Good People, but They Won't Have Ideas on How to Improve the Business

Many times, the best ideas come from the people who do the job every day. I look for ways to make my job better and easier. There are many other employees who do that, and there could be some in the business you manage.

Keep in mind that your employees could have good suggestions. It is their job and they may think of ways to do it more effectively. Let them know you appreciate their efforts. It's also good to recognize their attempts to help by telling your boss when your team members offer suggestions. Don't assume that everything they suggest will be great, but take the time to consider their input. Some of the best ideas come from employees.

### Give Complete Information

When you explain things to your employees, give them the full story. Giving them some of the details is not enough. It's like asking someone to assemble a puzzle with only half the pieces; there will be holes in the project. They need all the pieces to assemble the puzzle.

Incomplete information can cause employees to make wrong decisions. They need to make educated decisions, and this isn't possible without all of the details. The easiest way to fix this problem is to give them all the information you have. Share everything you know so they can do a complete job with complete information.

There will be some times when you need to hold back some

## MISTAKE #295
### If I Give the Employees All the Details, They Won't Need Me

This is a bad reason to hold back details. When you assign a project to an employee, he or she needs all the details you have in order to do it well. There could be some details you need to withhold due to privacy concerns, but everything that can be shared, needs to be shared.

information, but these are the only times you should keep information to yourself:

- Sensitive or confidential company information is involved. Managers need to know what details are sensitive and keep those confidential.

- If the information pertains to layoffs or other employees' issues. There are times when managers have advance information about layoffs and cannot share this information with their team members. When the time is right, the employees will be told about any company changes.

- If your boss has insisted that you keep certain information private. There may be times when you are confused about the reasoning and think it would be easier to give the employee the information. You might want to ask about your boss's thoughts if you think it would make a difference in the employee's performance.

Keep in mind that when you expect your employees to make

independent and accurate decisions, you need to give them enough information. Provide them with enough detail to make educated and effective decisions.

### The Art of Giving Constructive Criticism

There will be times when employees will make bad decisions. No matter how hard you work with them, it's still possible they will have problems. It's also possible that an employee might have done a job sufficiently but it didn't meet your expectations.

You must deal with situations that arise with employees. Tell them what they did wrong and give complete details on how to resolve the problem. It is beneficial to consider their viewpoint when you correct them. Shouting at them will not help the situation. Even if it makes you feel good at the time, it doesn't fix the problem.

When there is a problem, how should a boss respond? Here are some tips on how to deal with problems that arise with employee performance:

- Wait to see how the problem turns out.

---

### MISTAKE #296
#### I'll Ignore the Problem; It Might Go Away

Problems rarely, if ever, go away on their own. A more effective approach would be to face the problem head-on and help the employee improve.

---

- Reprimand the employee privately, never in public.

## MISTAKE #297
### All the Employees Need to Know This Was Wrong

It is good to let employees know when there is a problem, but you need to reprimand people in private.

- Explain what was done wrong.

## MISTAKE #298
### I Shouldn't Need to Do Any More Than Pointing Out the Problem

That would be easier, but the employee can't improve if you don't explain the problem and help him or her learn how to improve. Employees need to receive thorough and helpful criticism in order to improve and overcome the problems.

- Figure out the problem and what caused it. You could then decide how to fix the problem and discuss this plan with the employee in order to ensure it doesn't happen again.

## MISTAKE # 299
### I'll Tell Them They Are Wrong and Point Out Someone Else's Work

This could help, but the constructive criticism needs to be applied to the particular situation. The best-case scenario is to evaluate the problem, figure out the cause, and discuss with the employee how to fix the problem. This is the most thorough and effective way to approach the situation.

These are all options, but some are much more effective than others. The final option is by far the most thorough. The other options could be the easy way out of a difficult situation.

Your employees cannot improve and do a better job if they don't know there is a problem and don't know how to fix it. You need to let employees know exactly what is wrong and offer guidance and feedback to help them improve. This isn't that difficult and will make ongoing work better for you and your staff. Helpful and useful criticism is critical to help them improve.

### MISTAKE #300
#### I'll Tell Them There's a Problem; They Will Know What It Is

There's a slim chance this will work. You also need to remember that they may think something else is wrong. It is more effective to explain what the problem is and deal with it directly.

Your view of constructive criticism can make a huge difference in how it is received. If you feel negatively about giving suggestions, that is probably how the employee will perceive them. It is important that you develop a positive way to give criticism, without being confrontational. If you present the information is a sensitive and tactful way, you are likely to get positive results.

Think about any manager who gave you harsh or useless criticism about something you did. Was it helpful? Did it motivate you to do better? I've gotten that kind of criticism and it didn't help me improve. It created bad feelings about the manager and made it difficult to work together. You need to temper your comments with kindness and show employees that you want to help them. That is the key to making it work.

> ## *MISTAKE #301*
> ### *I Want to Get This Over so I Will Rush Through and Hit the Main Points Quickly*
>
> Rushing through your constructive criticism will give the impression that you are in a hurry and don't think it's worth your time to do this the right way. Show your employees that they deserve to be treated fairly.

The way you deliver criticism will also affect how it is received. When you deliver any criticism in a bad way, you risk making the recipient angry and defensive. This isn't the reaction you want, so you need to deliver it in a helpful and positive way.

Remember that the information and criticism you share will help employees become better at their jobs. That will benefit both of you. Keeping this in mind should help you get past your negative feelings about criticism. When it is given in the right way, and for the right reasons, it can be very effective.

> ## *MISTAKE #302*
> ### *My Employees Hate It When I Offer Criticism*
>
> There could be a couple of reasons for this. It could be the way you give criticism or you may be criticizing at inappropriate times. Two of the main reasons for criticism are to improve the quality of the job that is done and to help the employee improve. When criticism is handled properly, it helps your team members to do a better job and to fine-tune their skills and abilities.

When the need arises to point out the problems to your employees, it is also important to mention something positive. No matter how bad the situation is, there should be something positive that you can share. Don't let the positive comments overshadow the negatives they need to hear, but the good comments will temper the criticism.

Your employees need to understand that you value them and want them to improve and succeed. These are wonderful and positive reasons to offer effective and constructive criticism. Before you offer any criticism, take a few minutes to think about what to say and how to say it.

It's also good to have a plan in mind before you approach the employee. Make some notes about what you plan to say, if needed. Here are a few things you might mention:

- What went wrong?

- Was the assignment too much for the employee?

- Did they exhibit an attitude or behavior that you didn't like?

- What did you want or need the employee to do?

- How can the problem be solved?

- What needs to be done differently the next time?

- What has the employee done right?

When you approach the employee with these specifics, it shows him or her that you thought in detail about what happened. You are also providing input on how to fix the problem and keep it from happening again. These are important for you and for your team.

## CHOOSING THE BEST TYPE OF COMMUNICATION

In the twenty-first century, there are a wide variety of ways to communicate. We still have postal mail, e-mail, voice mail, phone calls, fax messages, and face-to-face communication. Each of these forms of communication has its own positives and negatives. We will discuss each and then you can make an educated decision on which form to use.

> ## *MISTAKE #303*
> ### *The Way I Choose to Send Messages Doesn't Make Any Difference*
>
> There are many ways to send and receive messages. Some are better for different people and situations.

### Postal Mail

Positive—"Snail" mail gives you time to think about what you want to say. It is your handwriting, and that appeals to many people.

Negative—It is slow and can be undependable if you address it wrong. It can take weeks or months to find out communications was sent to the wrong address.

### E-Mail

Positive—This is quick and very handy for people who are on the computer a lot. There are many free e-mail options, and some people have numerous e-mail accounts in order to keep various messages separate.

Negative—It is easy to be misinterpreted when you write things. This can happen when we rush through our messages, and many people rush through e-mails. Some people refuse to learn to use e-mail correctly.

### Phone Calls

Positives—Phone calls are a very effective way to communicate. Many times, you can speak with someone right away. On the telephone, you can hear what the person thinks and the sound of his or her voice. Some people don't like being stuck on the phone, but it is a great way to communicate effectively.

Negatives—There are times when you cannot get through to the person with whom you need to speak. Another downside is trying to speak with someone who is distracted or doing other things, although you can ask to talk at a different time if the person you're calling is busy.

### Voice Mail

Positive—Voice mail is a wonderful option when you call and the person isn't available. A nice touch in voice mail is that the person can hear your tone and inflection when you speak. This is missing in all written communication.

Negative—I've heard many voice mail messages that people left in a hurry, without thinking about what they were saying. Once you leave the message, it cannot be removed until the person checks their messages, so you need to be careful about what you say.

### Fax Messages

Positives—Fax machines are a simple and quick way to send written messages and documents. This is very helpful when you have the document in front of you or if the files aren't on your computer.

Negatives—Fax machine toner can be costly, and many businesses send junk faxes. Unlike e-mail, you may also have to pay long- distance charges for faxes.

### Face-to-Face Communication

Positives—Face-to-face is the best possible way to communicate for most people. Facing the person you are speaking with allows you to see the person, hear what he or she has to say, read his or her body language, and listen to the sound of his or her voice. If you are trying to explain a mistake or need to convince someone to do something, face-to-face communication is the most effective method. Discipline needs to be handled in person, and face-to-face is also good for your initial meeting with people.

Negatives—Some people do not like to talk in person. It doesn't allow a lot of time to compose your thoughts and ideas. You also need to be concerned about your appearance and behavior when you are in front of a business acquaintance.

It is very good for you to keep these alternatives in mind when you need to get in touch with someone. Are there some people you prefer to deal with in a specific way? Different people respond in a variety of ways, and it's good to respect other people's preferences.

## DEALING WITH QUESTIONS

Questions are an everyday part of a manager's life. Your boss and employees will come to you with questions. You can lose their respect and cooperation if you don't handle their questions appropriately.

> ### MISTAKE #304
> ### I Don't Know Any Answers Yet, so I'll Ignore Their Questions
>
> It is even more critical that you make an effort to find the answers. Don't just ignore your employees; tell them you don't have the answers, but you will find them.

Learning to ask and answer questions properly is critical for effective managers. You may need details about the business or the department. In order to get the details you want, you may need to ask different types of questions. We'll discuss the techniques to get the information you need.

### *Learn to Ask Questions—The Right Way*

The way you ask a question will determine what sort of answer you will receive. If you sound mad, the employee will become defensive. In turn, if you sound pleasant, he or she will be likely to respond in a positive and helpful manner. Avoid tones or words that seem adversarial or accusatory.

---

### *MISTAKE #305*
### *How I Ask Questions*
### *Doesn't Make Any Difference*

The words and tone you use makes a lot of difference in the responses that you get. You can help team members realize that you really want to help them, or you can make them feel that you are interrogating them.

---

Do you provide an atmosphere that is conducive to honesty? Make it possible for your employees to give you honest answers without worrying about repercussions. Help them understand that a person can be honest without being rude.

There are many things you can learn from skillfully asking questions, including the following:

- What is going on in the business or department and why.

- Critical insights into activities in and around the business or department.

- How you and your employees can do a better job.

- Deeper insights into what your employees are thinking.

Effective managers need to know and understand their employees. You must communicate in order to understand them. Take time to decide what you want to know and then figure out how to get those answers.

This can work the same way you would plan a trip. You know where you want to finish: at the answer. Once the answer is clear in your mind, figure what you need to do to get to that answer. If you begin that trek with no plan, you may wander around the questions endlessly before you reach the answer.

> # MISTAKE #306
> ## I've Always Thought All Questions Are Alike
>
> It may seem that way, but there are different types of questions. The types of questions you should ask depends on the type of information you need.

### The Types of Questions

Some questions are meant to clarify a point, while others will help expand your understanding of facts or issues. The questions you use depend on what you want to learn. What information do you need? Do you need a simple answer or a more complicated and involved answer? These explanations will help you understand how to tackle various questions.

- Questions for clarification and confirmation—These questions begin with "can," "do," "is," "will," "when," "who," and "did." Normally these questions will lead to "yes" or "no" answers or other short answers. You aren't asking for a lot of details when you use these questions. These are called "closed" questions.

- Questions for additional clarification—These questions begin with "how," "what," and "why." Answers to these questions require more detailed answers and more thought and effort. In turn, they will give you more information. These are not the types of questions to ask if a "yes" or "no" answer will really satisfy you.

- Questions that expand the response — Some questions allow you to dig deeper in order to mine for details. These should be used after you get simple or partial answers to your other questions.

When someone gives you a partial answer to a question, ask further questions by repeating a portion of their answers. This is also very helpful when the answer is too broad. You can narrow the focus by repeating the portion of the answer that pertains to the information you need to know. Also, remember to follow up on the answer. If there were details that the employee left out or if you need to zero-in on specific facts, then ask additional questions until you are satisfied.

One of the most important things is to remain positive when you ask questions. Even if you become frustrated, you need to keep an even tone and remain calm. You may be tempted to be sneaky with your employees, but that won't help you in the long run.

## MISTAKE #307
### I Tried to Find the Answer I Need, but I'm Losing Patience

This can happen if the person isn't giving you the answer you want. Take another look at the list above. If you aren't getting the right answers, try a different type of question. You might want one that will require the person to give a more detailed answer. Some questions dig deeper than others.

A basic principle in communication is to maintain eye contact when you speak to anyone. This is especially true when you need information from the person you're talking with. Have you ever talked to someone who avoids your eyes and looks everywhere else? Do you get the feeling he or she is hiding something? Your employees will feel the same way if you avoid eye contact.

Maintaining eye contact will show you care about them and are being honest. When you give them your attention, they will give you their attention in return.

> ## MISTAKE #308
> ### I Prefer to Look at My Notes When I Question People
>
> This could give the impression that you want to hide something, even if you don't. Looking a person in the eye is more personal and shows you are being honest.

It is good to make simple notes when you are talking to an employee. This shows the importance of the information. But be careful not to get so involved in your notes that you appear to be ignoring the person you're talking with. You also need to remain open. Is there anything you are doing that would make it seem as though you are collecting evidence against the employee?

When you ask a specific question, does the employee give you an unusual answer? Is the response confusing to you? This could be an indicator that your question wasn't worded well. If the question is confusing, the answer it elicits could also be confusing. In this case, you need to find another way to ask for the information you need.

> ## MISTAKE #309
> ### The Team Member Is Giving Me the Wrong Answer
>
> Take a close look at the answers the employee is giving you. This could be an indication that you are asking the wrong questions. Try rewording your questions and see what type of responses you get.

The better you get with your questioning, the more comfortable your employees should be with you. Make your employees feel comfortable, and you should gain more useful information. They will hold back information when they are uncomfortable.

Effective questioning is a skill that you will need to practice. It is not natural for most people, but with practice you can talk with your employees and gain the information you need. Sometimes you only need to approach the team member from a different angle. These skills will also help you work around and past the vague answers, but be cautious at first. Build and improve your skills and you will be more effective.

### Answer Employees' Questions

In the beginning, employees often bombard new managers with questions. The employees should know that you haven't been there long enough to know all the answers. They may be testing you to see how you will handle that. You need to find the answers for them. Your boss would be a great place to begin looking for the answers.

> # MISTAKE #310
> ## I Have to Make Up an Answer for Their Questions
> This is a bad idea. Take the time to find the right answer. You will earn respect if you are honest and admit you don't have the answer.

You are the person who represents the company to your employees, so they will bring their questions to you. Remember that personal problems and questions will affect their morale. Job-related problems and questions impact their productivity. Both of these issues will affect your life at work. It's your responsibility to maintain their morale and productivity.

Various questions affect employees in different ways. Here are some examples:

1. **Everyday questions**

- Answer these questions right away if possible.

- If you resolved a similar question, you might be able to use the same solution.

## MISTAKE #311
### I'll Ignore Their Questions When I Don't Know the Answers

Your employees will be too savvy for this behavior. Don't think they will let you get away with this.

2. **New procedural questions**

- Workers may not be familiar with new job procedures and policies.

- You will probably need input from your boss to answer these questions.

## MISTAKE #312
### They Can't Expect Me to Know Those Answers

If you don't know the details of new procedures, you need to find out who can answer these questions for your employees. Uncertainty about how to do their jobs will decrease your team members' productivity.

3. **Personnel questions**

- There will be questions when pay and benefits change.

- You should talk to human resources or your boss for answers.

- If they affect everyone, call a meeting and announce the changes.

## MISTAKE #313
### It's a Little Change in Vacation Policy, It's Not a Big Deal

Changes in benefits are a big deal to your employees. Any change in pay or benefits will affect employees, and you need to find the answers quickly.

4. **Difficult questions**

- You may need to find an expert to answer some questions.

- When you have someone else answer questions, follow up with employee to ensure all their questions were answered.

## MISTAKE #314
### That Question Is Too Hard; I Can't Find an Answer

That may be true, but it's rare. There's usually someone with an answer. Talk to your boss or other supervisors to get advice about who to ask. You need to find an answer.

5. **Personal Concerns**

- You need to evaluate each question on a case-by-case basis.

- It may be necessary to do research and get back to the employee.

- There may not be an answer. If so, you must explain that to the employee.

## MISTAKE #315
### There Isn't an Answer, but I Can't Tell

On the rare occasion when there isn't an answer, you have to be honest with your employee. But be sure that you have exhausted every possibility to find an answer.

### Listen to Employees' Questions

There are times when it is tempting to cut people short when they are asking questions. However, you shouldn't do this to your employees. They need to feel comfortable and confident when talking to you. The best way to handle this is to focus on their question and help them as quickly as possible.

---

## MISTAKE #316
### When My Employees Have Questions, I Can Just Nod in Response

Let your employees know that you are concerned about them. This requires eye contact and interaction with your employees in order to help them know you are concerned about them and want to help them.

---

Employees will ask you questions for many reasons. They may need your help or reassurance about their concerns. Perhaps they want to make sure that you are aware of them or that you know your job well. In any case, it's important for you to listen to their questions and answer them accurately. Here are just a few of the reasons why employees might approach you with questions:

1.  They need your help. Their questions could be legitimate requests for your help. You may feel that you aren't qualified to help them, but listen to their questions and then determine if you can find a way to be of assistance. It is best for you to help them, if you can. When you don't know the answer, you can ask someone else for help or you can refer employees to another person for assistance, but it is better for you to find someone to help instead of telling employees to ask around. This makes you look better to your employees and will also help you to find the answer to their question.

## MISTAKE #317
### Why Do My Employees Ask Me All Their Questions?

It is better for your employees to bring their questions to you. We talked in the beginning that you should discourage them from taking their questions to others. When they ask you how to do things, you can ensure they do the job the way you want.

2. Do you know your job? Employees might want to test your knowledge. If you don't know the answers, you need to search for them. There will be times when the employee should know the answer. Remember that you don't need to apologize for not knowing everything in the beginning. You will know much more about the business or department soon.

## MISTAKE #318
### I Don't Need to Prove Anything; I Got the Job

You did get the job, but you need to help your employees understand that you are qualified despite not knowing all the answers right away. Your qualifications will make a big difference in how the business or department is run, and your team will feel better if they understand that you know how to do the job.

3. Make themselves known. Your employees may come to you with questions, but it could be a ploy to talk with you. They might take the chance to recite their experience. Take some time to talk with them, but don't let your other responsibilities slide. Once they feel that you understand their background, this shouldn't happen anymore.

> ## MISTAKE #319
> ### They Don't Need My Help;
> ### They Already Know the Answer
>
> This could be true, but they might be trying to get your attention. Maybe the employee feels insecure and just needs to make sure you know he or she is in the department or business. This can be especially true when you have a lot of employees. Some people feel lost in the shuffle and want to speak with you personally.

4. Boost their confidence. Some employees need your reassurance that they are doing a good job. This can be irritating when they pester you, but you need to find a way to boost their confidence. Once they are confident about their job performance, this should stop.

> ## MISTAKE #320
> ### Jo Ellen Does a Good Job, but She Needs to Stop Coming to Me About Small Things
>
> Have you told Jo Ellen that she's doing a good job? This could make all the difference. Many times, the person just needs to hear they are doing well.

5. Are you willing to discuss problems? Employees may need to verify that you will discuss issues with them. They will find this out by asking you questions. How do you handle their questions and concerns? If you tell them you have an open-door policy, then you need to open your door when they have questions. You need to be careful that these discussions don't take up too much work time. Answer their questions and concerns directly, but don't let them take away from their productivity.

## MISTAKE #321
### I Don't Have Time to Talk to My Employees About Their Problems

With all of your management responsibilities, it can be tough to find time to discuss problems with your employees, but you want them to know that they can talk to you. Make sure to leave aside some time for answering your employees' questions.

Each of these reasons can have a different impact on your employees. Handle each carefully and thoroughly. Many times, your staff just need to know that you are satisfied with their work. If you aren't, then you need to speak with them in a tactful and helpful way to resolve the problem. All of these things will make your job as a manager better.

# CHAPTER 18

# Delegation

L earning to delegate effectively can make a big difference in the difficulty of your job. You have employees to help you do your job, but you need to utilize their abilities in the best way possible. There are jobs that you shouldn't delegate and people you shouldn't delegate to. One of the secrets is learning when to delegate work and whom to include.

Delegation is a complicated issue. One problem is that some people are unwilling to give up any control. Sometimes this is because they feel no one else can do the job as well. There have been times when I didn't delegate work because I knew it would take longer to explain the project than to do it myself. Another problem is that some people want to turn everything over to other people.

> ## MISTAKE #322
> ### I'm the Manager and I Have to Be in Charge of Everything
>
> That is the hard way to do the job. You have employees and it's best to learn how to utilize their skills and abilities. There are many tasks that you can delegate to your employees without having any problems.

One warning before we dive into the specifics of delegation: When you delegate improperly, it can increase your workload and decrease your effectiveness. I will give you tips to help you learn the art of effective delegation.

> ## MISTAKE #323
> ### I'll Delegate Everything Except Payroll
>
> There are tasks that you must handle yourself. An effective and respected manager does not delegate everything. You will learn to pick and choose which tasks can be delegated and which cannot.

## HOW TO DELEGATE

In order to know how to delegate a project, you need to fully understand its details. This will help you explain the specifics to a team member and also help you decide who would be the most qualified to handle the job.

> ## MISTAKE #324
> ### It's My First Week and I Need Help; I'll Just Assign Projects Based on Where Employees Sit
>
> That probably won't work. You need to find out some things about your employees before you delegate. This is hard in the beginning, but you can explain what is involved in the task. Look for positive reactions and volunteers.

In the beginning, you need to delegate work to others in order to get things done. This allows you additional time to learn what is required of you. The irony is that in the beginning, you don't know enough to delegate efficiently. You have no choice, though, and you will have to delegate tasks and learn from your mistakes. Your boss may be willing to give you some input about which employees would be best, but he may not know them well enough to give you the right answer. The fact that you asked him should help him realize you want to delegate effectively.

When you delegate to people you don't know very well, there are some things that can make it work better. One of these is to talk with the employees and explain the tasks to be done. Listen and watch their reactions. If they are negative or unsure, they are not the right people. Keep in mind that delegating to someone who is not qualified can make your job more difficult and make more work for you.

### MISTAKE #325
### I Really Need Someone to Step Up, but Since They Didn't, I'll Pick Julia Even Though She Seemed Negative About the Project

If you notice negative signals from an employee about a job, it isn't good to delegate the project to that person. It would be better to keep looking for someone else.

Your delegating skills will improve with practice and as you learn more about the job. Once you learn more about the skills your team members possess, you might realize that you have people who try to get out of additional work. They might be qualified, but they shy away from accepting assignments. Make a note about these occurrences for the employees' evaluations.

## MISTAKE #326
### I'll Never Learn to Delegate; It's Too Hard

It is hard in the beginning, but it does become easier over time. Learning the various facets of the job will help you find the right person for future projects. Learning more about your employees' strengths and weaknesses will also help you delegate better.

There will be other team members who want to pitch in and help you get work done. Working with them will help get the project completed and help you learn where their strengths lie. Also put a note in their employee files about the employees' willingness to help.

## MISTAKE #327
### I Could Ask Them What They Can Do Well

You can ask, but you also need to watch them. Some people like to exaggerate their skills; you need to know where their strengths really lie. Listen to their answers and watch their performance. This will give you a good idea of what they can actually do.

Whomever you delegate to, you need to follow their progress and the quality of the work. You will learn more by following up, and it is a great way to monitor their work to ensure it is done right. Even if the work is not done exactly like you want it, the extra help is a blessing, especially when you are new.

## MISTAKE #328
### Once I Find a Qualified and Willing Person, I Can Forget About the Project

You need a qualified and willing person, but then you also need to follow up and keep an eye on their progress. It's never good to assume the task is fine. Check on the team member and give your input when needed.

After you have been on the job for a while, you will have a better grasp on the work to be done and the employee qualifications. At this point, you need to become more effective in your delegating. Here are some tips to help you:

- When you assign a project, explain all the details to the employee and be sure he or she understands.

- Make sure the team member knows to come to you with any additional questions. If they have additional questions, you need to provide the answers.

> ### MISTAKE #329
> ### *I Explained All the Details;*
> ### *He Should Be Able to Handle It*
>
> There are almost always questions. Be sure the employee knows to bring questions to you. This helps you monitor the project and ensure that it's going well.

- The team member may need some additional authority to accomplish the task. You need to give them the proper direction to guarantee they can complete the project.

- Give a definite time frame for completion of the project. A large project should be divided into stages, with clear details on what is included in each stage and the time period that is expected for completion. If it is in-depth, you might want to have the employee initial the timeline to make sure you each understand and agree to the project terms.

## MISTAKE #330
### It's a Big Project; She Can Finish Anytime

This will leave things up in the air. You both need to have a definite time when the project should be complete. You can even set "milestones" within the project for progress reports.

- Give appropriate feedback on the work being done. This helps the employee know that you are in touch with the project and helps you stay on top of the details. If there are problems along the way, this enables you to head them off before they get out of control.

## MISTAKE #331
### I Will Give Him My Thoughts When He's Finished

If you notice problems or concerns, you need to let the employee know during the project. Even if the task is going well, you should be communicating with the person and getting regular updates.

There are some very definite pitfalls to avoid when you delegate. One of these is not explaining the details thoroughly. As we discussed in the previous chapter on communication, you should give employees all the details to enable them to do the job properly. When you assign projects, make sure that your employees understand what is expected of them.

Remember, even if you are familiar with the project, that doesn't mean that your employees know the specifics. Through the years, I have learned it's better to repeat something important than it is to miss something. Ask your employees if they have questions, or you can have them explain the project to you. Having them explain the details is a great way to be sure they understand.

**MISTAKE #332**
**I'm Pretty Sure She Has All the Details**

You should make sure that your employees have all the details. It's much better to repeat something than to be unsure about whether a team member has enough information.

## WHEN YOU SHOULD DELEGATE

When you consider who to delegate a project to, consider your employees' qualifications. Different people have different strengths and weaknesses. When you delegate, use those strengths and weaknesses to your advantage. It is better to fit the job to the employee than to force an unqualified person to take on a task that he or she simply isn't qualified to handle.

**MISTAKE #333**
**It Seems Like Some Employees Are Better at Different Things, but I Can't Use That**

This is a key point in delegation. You need to determine the strengths and weaknesses of your employees and then assign tasks based on those abilities. When you learn to match tasks with their talents, your job will go smoother and productivity will increase dramatically.

What if you have a person who has some of the strengths you need but needs to develop some additional skills? Does this person show initiative and a desire to learn? The task could be a good opportunity to help the team member expand his or her abilities. This is a case where you really need to follow up and monitor the progress. Your help can keep the employee on track and provide learning opportunities. The extra time now will make things easier for you in the long run.

## MISTAKE #334
### I Don't Want to Push a Willing Employee

When this situation arises, determine whether it is something the employee could do with some additional effort. It's good to challenge your team members, especially the ones who show initiative. Gauge their reactions to see how far you can nudge them. As long as they understand that you will be there to answer questions, they will usually be willing to try a more difficult project. To make this work, you need to match the right team member with the right project.

Some projects can always be delegated, but you need to consider other projects more carefully:

- Routine tasks can be delegated. Your employees can learn to do these well and can do them on a regular basis. Routine tasks are just "busy" work for you, and managers don't need "busy" work.

- Your more qualified team members can assume some of the tasks that require a lot of your time. Some large projects require a lot of time and it is better for you to delegate these, but be sure the team members are qualified to handle the job. Even though you trust the employees to do a good job, you still need to follow up.

## MISTAKE #335
### The Company Owner Asked Me to Do a Big Project, but I Don't Have Time

Look at the project. Is it something that you could delegate to someone else? This could be a great way to get additional work done and leave you free to do other tasks. You could also manage the project yourself and delegate portions to your employees.

What qualities and abilities does an employee need? That depends to some degree on the task you want to delegate. This is when you need to evaluate employees' strengths and weaknesses to find the most qualified person for the project. Here are some of the abilities you will notice:

- Some people excel at projects that involve detail work.

- Others will turn out a lot of work, but the quality may be lower.

> ## MISTAKE #336
> ### I Have a Rush Project and My Most Qualified Person Is Really Slow
>
> If you have a project that needs to be done in a hurry, you wouldn't assign it to a person who labors over every detail. You want the job to be done well, but you also need to consider the turnaround time.

Your team needs to be productive. How can you ensure your team's productivity? One way is by knowing the talents of your individual team members. That will enable you to utilize their skills in the best place. When a person is assigned to a task that requires their strong points, things go smoothly and productivity soars.

> ## MISTAKE #337
> ### I Can Count on Harvey, so I Need to Assign A Lot of Tasks to Him
>
> Even though you can trust Harvey, it isn't good to overburden him. You need to spread the tasks between employees. This will ensure that you don't take advantage of your best people and will keep them from getting burned out.

Another important thing to keep in mind is that you shouldn't overburden your best people. In tough situations, it's easier to gravitate to the people who do the best work. However, that can put too much work on them.

## WHEN YOU SHOULDN'T DELEGATE

There are some people who simply cannot handle additional responsibilities. Some team members are happy with routine assignments and don't want to do more. You shouldn't delegate to these types of people. At times, there are team members who want to usurp your authority. You shouldn't give them that added responsibility.

### MISTAKE #338
#### Helen Doesn't Want Extra Responsibility and Can't Handle Her Current Workload, but Maybe Delegating More Would Motivate Her

If a person cannot handle his or her everyday job, then don't delegate more work. You need to pick team members carefully before you delegate anything to them. Helen might be a nice person, but she isn't a candidate for this project.

Another common pitfall is to delegate a project and then to avoid any follow up or supervision. Just because a team member is heading up a project, it doesn't mean that you don't need to be involved. You are still ultimately responsible for the outcome of the task.

> ## *MISTAKE #339*
> ### *Joel Is Great and I Don't Need to Follow Up on Projects That I Delegate to Him*
>
> Even though you don't think you need to check on him, it's still a good idea. Take a few opportunities to see how the project is going. You could ask some insightful questions and get a feel for how the project is going.

There will be tasks that need the authority of the manager. While you can give temporary authority for some projects, don't assign tasks that you need to handle personally. When you delegate these tasks to someone else, you send the message that they aren't important enough for you to bother with. This will cause problems on many levels, including your client, your boss, and employees.

I'll give you a simple list of indicators to help you decide if something should be delegated to another person. If you answer "yes" to these questions, then the assignment should not be delegated.

- Does someone with higher authority need to handle the task? This could include an important client or confidential matter.

- Does it involve critical work with suppliers, clients, supervisors, or the media? These projects need your attention.

> ## *MISTAKE #340*
> ### *There Might Be Confidentiality Issues, but I Can Trust Gerry*
>
> Being able to trust an employee isn't enough. Some issues in a business must be kept among the supervisors and cannot be delegated to someone else.

- Is there a significant risk to the business? Assignments that could cause major problems shouldn't be delegated.

- Will the employee need to give direction to other team members? You need your employees to come to you for instruction. It is not good to have other employees give direction to team members. This will give them the impression you feel like you're too important to talk to them directly. You probably don't think that, but it can seem that way to your employees.

### MISTAKE #341
### I Don't Feel Right About Delegating This Project, but I Need to Do It Anyway

If you feel wrong about delegating a project, then look more closely at it before you give the project away. Make sure that it's an appropriate assignment to delegate, and be sure that you're handing the project to an employee who will get it done.

If you have a bad feeling about a delegation decision, then it's probably a bad idea. Some people have great gut instincts, and you should listen to those feelings. This is like many other things in management: The decisions become easier over time. Most of your responsibilities will be difficult in the beginning, but as you learn your job and your employees' abilities, these will become easier.

## HELPING TEAM MEMBERS TAKE RISKS

There is a common phrase about staying in your "comfort zone." You probably have employees who don't want to venture past their "comfort zones." Others may welcome a challenge and want to improve themselves. When you find people who are willing to take risks, encourage them. People can improve themselves by taking risks and pushing the boundaries of their "comfort zones."

## MISTAKE #342
### Lori Isn't Comfortable with the Project and That's a Shame; She Would Be Great

If Lori hasn't proven herself, then you should approach her again about handling something that would stretch her talents. You might mention that it would help her grow and become more valuable to the company. Only push the employees if you feel sure they can handle added responsibility.

When you encourage employees to take risks, you also need to follow up and watch their progress. This enables you to help them avoid problems. A successful project will encourage them to take more risks, and they can be a big help to you. You can help employees feel confident by allowing them to come to you with problems and questions.

## MISTAKE #343
### I Convinced Sara to Take the Project; Now I Don't Have to Think About it

You still need to follow-up and make sure the project is going well. This is especially critical with risky and difficult projects. Remember that your team's performance reflects on you. Give them the help they need to succeed.

Part of your job involves helping your team members take on additional responsibilities. This helps them to grow and improve their job performance. Delegating will help them feel more secure about their performance and more likely to take risks.

You can help employees expand their abilities by working on different types of projects. Employees can get in a rut with the tasks they do. It's good for them to do different projects and learn new things. You can encourage employees to take chances by making sure they have a "safety net." Keep the risks within reason and find challenging projects that suits their skills.

While you want your team members to spread their wings and learn more, you don't want to increase your potential for risk. Here are a few ways to prevent that problem:

- Give employees complete and sufficient information.

- Provide the necessary resources to complete the project.

- Make sure employees have the support they need to do the task.

- Follow up on their progress with the project.

You should also ask yourself several questions before you assign a risky task. These will help you ensure that you made the right decision.

- Does the employee have the skills the task requires?

- Does he or she have good decision-making skills?

- Will the employee be able to handle potential problems?

These are basic questions that will zero-in on whether a particular person is qualified to handle the job. If you are satisfied, then assign the project and help the team member to grow.

We produced a product line of high-speed printers. We had finished our newest and best model. It would be introduced at the upcoming computer show.

A new brochure was prepared with a picture of the product and listed the specifications.

The general manager decided to change the picture of the product, but he never told the Engineering Department. He wanted the data terminal to be shown in red. This gave an appealing look on the product brochure. This was an easy change for Marketing.

Well, we introduced the product at the computer show. It was a good high-performance machine and our Sales department took orders for it. One of the early customers ordered 12. When they arrived, he called the Sales Department and said, "They are OK, but aren't red as shown in the brochure." The customer said he'd been sold red machines, so he returned the products.

Our Engineering Department modified drawings to build red machines. Manufacturing built 12 for the customer and an additional red machine for our product display room.

When the general manager saw the red machine on display, he had it removed and put away. It was a big embarrassment to him. No one ever said anything about it for fear of what the general manager might do.

Anonymous

One of the biggest mistakes I've made in my business is to not delegate tasks. The other big mistake I've made is to delegate the wrong tasks. It often seems like a vicious circle. Over the last five years, I fought tooth and nail against assigning tasks to others because I ultimately believed the task was not completed properly or good enough. Having a few perfectionist tendencies, I never believed anyone could do anything as well as I could, so I tried to do everything myself—HUGE mistake. I rarely got things done, and if I did, I was never pleased with the result.

I have learned that the most effective way to get things done is to delegate the task and then communicate to that person how I would like it done. I am learning to maintain better communication so when there are concerns or questions, I am available. I never imagined that being an effective leader would mean letting others do the things I felt most responsible for. By building better working relationships, the people I delegate to share my level of enthusiasm. They understand and respect the standards I have set and they are eager and willing to work with me to reach those goals.

Karen L. Syed, President
Echelon Press Publishing
**www.echelonpress.com**

# Motivation

**M**otivating your employees is important to maintaining morale and good performance with your team members. We have all known unmotivated employees who dread coming to work and have bad attitudes when they get there. This is an unpleasant situation for everyone.

A motivated employee will work harder for you. This improves the situation for everyone on your team. A pleasant and hard-working crew will also make your job easier. There are many positives to having a motivated team. So the next logical question would be, "How can I motivate my team?"

# CREATE AND MAINTAIN POSITIVE ATTITUDES

When I mention "attitude," what comes to your mind? I'm talking about your state of mind and how you feel about something. This is what influences the way you do things and how you feel about that task. When you have a predisposition about a subject, it can affect your attitude about related or similar subjects.

---

### MISTAKE #344
### *I'm Not Excited About the Project, but I'll Get It Done*

If you have negative feelings about a project, they will carry over to your performance. Your team members will notice if you don't like the project.

---

There are a series of things that will influence your attitude, including the following:

- What you tell yourself about something will affect how you react. If you tell yourself something good, then you will feel positive. In turn, when you tell yourself something bad, you will feel negative. So you have the power to feel good or bad about something.

- Your state of mind will have an impact. Keep in mind that this is affected by what you tell yourself.

  Attitude = thoughts and feelings

- How do you react to your feelings? This shows how interdependent these elements are.

Our thoughts are often more powerful than we realize. If you tell yourself that you don't like something or can't do something, it will cause you to avoid it. This type of thinking is very powerful and will have a definite impact on productivity.

### MISTAKE #345
#### I Cannot Lead This Project

This is an issue of mind over matter. You could learn more about the project and the subject. Ask your boss for some additional information if that would help you. You need to do the same thing when your team members have doubts about themselves.

Positive and negative attitudes are powerful, so let's identify some of these:

- Positive—Sincere caring or love. These promote helpful and beneficial actions.

- Negative—Fear and anger, whether there is a basis for it or not. These lead to hurtful and defensive actions.

This makes it pretty clear which attitudes and thoughts you need with your team members. Negativity, hurtfulness, and defensiveness cause bad attitudes and limit productivity. It is critical that you find ways to motivate your team and to avoid negativity that could squelch productivity.

### MISTAKE #346
#### A Couple of My Team Members Are Really Negative, but I Don't Think It Will Hurt Anyone Else

Attitudes are usually contagious. This seems to be especially true with negative attitudes. When you find employees who are negative, you need to deal with their attitudes right away.

Maintaining a positive attitude helps the overall morale of the employees. Have you worked with someone who is unhappy at work? It can ruin a great day. Even when you are working hard and things are going great, a disgruntled team member can make work a chore.

## MISTAKE #347
### I Had a Great Weekend and Nothing Can Ruin My Morning

That probably isn't true. When you come to work and you have to deal with unhappy team members, it will bring you down. You can help them cheer up with your positive attitude, but unfortunately the negative thoughts usually prevail.

It's important that you maintain a good attitude. Bad attitudes are contagious, especially when the boss is negative. Be enthusiastic about the task at hand.

## MISTAKE #348
### I Hope My Employees Don't Notice I'm in a Bad Mood

They usually do. No matter how hard I tried to hide a bad mood, my long-time employees always knew. I would strive to cheer up and they were encouraging. It's wonderful when you can cheer each other up, but it's better to lose the bad mood before you get to work.

Showing an interest in your team members also promotes positive attitudes. Let them know that you care about them. Ask about their kids or give them a birthday or anniversary card. Maybe you could let them go home a couple hours early for a child's birthday. There are many things you can do that could mean a lot to them and prove that you understand they are human beings with lives outside the office.

## MISTAKE #349
### I Don't Need to Know About My Employees' Personal Lives

You don't have to, but they will be encouraged by the fact that you care about them. This shows your employees that you realize they have lives outside of work.

This has been mentioned before, but it can be repeated. Ask your team for their suggestions. They like to know that you want their opinions and it helps them feel more involved.

## MISTAKE #350
### My Team Members Wouldn't Have Any Suggestions

You don't know this unless you ask them. It doesn't hurt to ask and then to listen to their thoughts. Some wonderful ideas come from employees. No one knows their job better than they do. Utilize that knowledge to make everyone's job easier. You can motivate them by appreciating their ideas and recognizing their contributions.

One of the hardest things to accept is that there are many ways to motivate your team. There isn't a one-step quick fix, but the little things add up and help to motivate your employees.

## MISTAKE #351
### This Motivating Thing Is Easy; I'll Pick One Thing to Do and They Will Be Motivated

Motivation is harder and more involved than that. It requires an ongoing effort on your part. You need to show appreciation and support on a regular basis.

# MOTIVATION PROMPTS PRODUCTIVITY

One benefit to motivating your team members is that it increases their productivity. There are many benefits to a productive team, and your boss will take notice. When your team members accomplish a lot, that takes pressure off you and makes your job easier.

## MISTAKE #352
### I Wish There Was a Way That Motivating Would Help Me

There are ways it helps you. It can make your job easier because employees are more productive when they are motivated to work hard and to do a good job. This makes you look good and helps your team get their work done.

Are there any simple ways to increase their productivity? Here are some tips that will help you:

- There will be problems in the business or department from time to time. Encourage your employees to offer solutions. You might get some ideas you can use or you might not. Either way, you involved your staff and indicated that you value their opinions and thoughts.

## MISTAKE #353
### I Asked for Suggestions and It Didn't Do Any Good

Even if they didn't have any useful ideas, it was still successful. You motivated them by involving them and showing that you want to hear their thoughts.

- Some people like to have departmental competitions, but avoid setting employees against each other in a negative way. You want to build a team, and these things can cause divisions in your department.

## MISTAKE #354
### My Team Needs a Good Competition

The idea is to build a team that will support each other and work well together. You can undo that by having your employees compete and work against one another.

- Always be on the lookout for ways to make the job easier and to streamline procedures. These ideas can be entirely new ways to do the job or ways to improve current procedures. This increases productivity because the jobs will go faster and more smoothly.

## MISTAKE #355
### Malik Has an Idea About His Job; It Probably Won't Help

Don't assume it won't work. There will probably be at least some part of his idea that will make his job easier. That will motivate and encourage him. Motivated and happy employees work harder and accomplish more, so listen to their ideas.

- Help your team members to understand the importance of maintaining and increasing productivity. You could even do special things for your team members based on their work or reward unique ideas that save work and promote productivity.

## MISTAKE #356
### I Feel Like I'm The Only One Concerned with Productivity

Helping your team members understand how increased productivity helps everyone can change that. It will help them look better to the boss. This takes the pressure off because more work is being done and the supervisors are happy. It can also help because productive employees are worth more money to their employers.

- I always train my employees to handle multiple tasks. When I interview, I also let them know that employees are more valuable when they can do more facets of the job.

## MISTAKE #357
### I Want People Who Can Multitask, but It Might Be Better to Tell Them After They Accept the Job

If you plan to require your employees to multitask and to cross-train on different jobs, tell them in the beginning. This requires extra effort, and they need to be told in their interviews. That will help you weed out the people who aren't willing to follow your guidelines.

## AVOID SHOWING FAVORITISM

Showing favoritism can cause many problems within your business. The reason that is critical in this chapter is because having favorites will "unmotivate" people. As a manager, you expend the time and effort to motivate your staff, and showing favoritism can undo the good.

You expect loyalty from your team members, and they expect the same from you. Supporting your employees is one way to show your loyalty. When you show favoritism that is undeserved, you are betraying the other people in the department.

## MISTAKE #358
### June Is Showing a Bad Attitude and I Need to Turn That Around; a Reward Might Help Her Improve

You never want to reward people who don't deserve it. You will also set a bad precedent with your team. It gives them the idea that they don't need to work hard to get something special. And, finally, it will discourage people who are working hard from doing their jobs.

Most people understand their performance determines their success with the company. When they see certain employees getting preferential treatment, it undermines their motivation. It appears that they won't be rewarded for their hard work and will lose some of their motivation to do the best job possible.

A little favoritism for some employees may not seem like a big deal, but it can have negative repercussions. Do you want to risk that in your business? One way to avoid that is to be sure you can substantiate any favoritism that you show. There are good reasons to favor certain employees. This could include doing an outstanding job on a project, developing a new process for tasks, or doing something else that benefits the company and your team.

## MISTAKE #359
### There Isn't Any Good Reason to Recognize Scott, but I Want to Do It Anyway

Your team will see this as undeserved favoritism. When you give recognition that is undeserved, you leave the door open for problems and bad feelings from other employees. Any time you recognize an employee, you should have a solid reason for your actions.

A way to protect yourself from unfair accusations is to be sure you have some justification for the favoritism before you recognize employees. If you cannot justify it to yourself, there is no chance that your employees will believe you.

When you recognize employees for doing their job well, it will motivate them to continue to do well and it can motivate others to work harder. Recognition and proper favoritism can be very motivating. Just be sure that it is warranted.

## ENCOURAGE IMPROVEMENT

Managers always like to see their employees improve. Employee improvement can mean better productivity. A great way to encourage employees to improve is by motivating them. Most people want to do better, and your encouragement can make a big difference.

### MISTAKE #360
#### It's Hard to Believe People Want to Do Better

It may be hard to believe, but it is true. Many people want to do a good job, and there is a "rush" from knowing they did a job well. I've always felt great after completing a job, especially a difficult one. There is such a feeling of accomplishment when a complicated job is done well. Help your employees strive for this satisfaction.

People try to do better when they know someone will support them. Show support for your team members and show that you will be available when they have a problem. This can motivate them to take chances and help them improve. As they improve, they become more valuable to you and the business.

If an employee comes to you about something they don't know, how do you handle it? Would you help him or her learn more, or shrug it off and have someone else do the work? When employees come to you about a task, it is probably because they want to improve their skills. Remember that your employees can become bored if you don't challenge them and encourage them to do more. Offering to help your employees improve is very motivating. They want to do more and you can help them. This will help them be more interested and motivate them to continue to strive for more.

## MISTAKE # 361

### Bridget Said She Doesn't Understand Part of the Task; I'll Assign It to Someone Else

This would be a wonderful opportunity to help Bridget learn more and to excel. Take some time to delve into the questions with her so she can handle the situation alone the next time it happens. If you reassign the work, that discourages the employees who have to clean up or complete Bridget's work.

If you have time before the work is due, work with employees to help them learn the additional skills to complete the project. This will encourage them to strive to do and learn more. They will understand that you want them to succeed and will work harder for you. This is a wonderful way to motivate the employee.

Cross-training and multitasking are ways to encourage your team members to do more and will increase productivity within the department. Having people who can do multiple jobs is a great thing for you when there is a problem or an overload of work to be done. These employees are worth more to you and the company and they should be encouraged to excel.

## MISTAKE #362
### *I Hear a Lot About Multitasking, but It Sounds Like Too Much Trouble for My Team*

There is work involved in training people to handle multiple tasks on the job. However, the potential benefits far outweigh the work that is needed. Once your employees learn more skills, they are more valuable and you have more flexibility when its time to assign projects.

Listen to your employees when they want to do more. If they want additional responsibilities, encourage them. Are there training seminars they can attend? Is there someone they can work with to learn more? Find solutions quickly and keep their momentum going. These are all ways to encourage and motivate your staff.

Another facet of this is to recognize employees who excel. There will be some team members who do a consistently good job. Do you take their work for granted? Or, do you tell them that you appreciate their work? It is your responsibility to be sure they know their efforts are appreciated.

## MISTAKE #363
### *I Can Count on Some Employees to Do a Great Job Every Time; I Don't Have to Check on Them or Think About Them*

It's wonderful that you have employees who are so dependable. Even though you don't have to worry about them, do you take time to thank them for their superior work? Unfortunately, it is very easy to take this sort of employee for granted. You may be overwhelmed with problems and forget to show your appreciation. It is important that you take time to recognize the things they do. You do not want these productive people to lose their motivation to do an outstanding job.

The best employees get tired of being taken for granted. I've seen this happen with employees who aren't told they are appreciated. The owners or managers do appreciate them, but they need to convey that to the employees. Never just assume that an employee knows you appreciate him or her. That is not enough. Tell the team member on a regular basis that he or she is appreciated. Make your employees feel wanted. This will motivate them to continue to do a consistent and superior job.

When you notice that employees did a good job, take the opportunity to praise their work. This is a natural follow up to their performance. Don't think they will get tired of being praised; they won't. If they do an outstanding job five days in a row, tell them you appreciate that effort each day. It takes very little effort to say "thank you" and "good job," but you will reap the rewards by motivating your team.

I've heard it said that a good manager is a cheerleader, and it's true. It is your job to oversee your team members, but also to encourage them. You need to be the first person to recognize their performance and to cheer for them. Make them feel appreciated and you will notice their motivation.

## BELOW AVERAGE WORK

You can destroy morale and ruin motivation by allowing substandard work. When your employees do substandard work, you need to address the situation. You need the employees' performance to remain consistent. This requires that you deal with work that does not meet your standards.

## MISTAKE #364
### Tony's Work Is Substandard, but I Can Have Someone Else Fix It

This doesn't help anyone. The employee who is doing substandard work doesn't improve and develops the idea that he or she can get away with low-quality work. You will also cause problems with the employees who have to clean up the work. It is more effective to help Tony improve. This can motivate everyone involved.

The first priority is to explain your expectations to your team. Be sure they understand the standards that you insist they maintain. They cannot work up to your requirements unless they understand them. Every manager must set standards for their employees' performance.

Explain the quality of work that you need from your team. If they have questions, give them a complete explanation and help them understand what is required of them. When they do well, motivate them by recognizing their successes. Point out what you liked about their work. If others hear, it will improve their performance as well.

## MISTAKE #365
### I Want High-Quality Work, but Don't Want to Push My Team

You have to make your standards known to your employees. It's unreasonable to insist they meet your expectations if you didn't tell them what you want. Be clear and direct about what you expect from your team members and give them advice on how to reach their goals.

When an employee does less than you expect, explain how to fix the existing problems. The team member will learn more if you have them make the changes. If someone else fixes the mistakes, the original employee doesn't learn or improve. This will discourage both employees and doesn't motivate anyone.

You need to explain problems to your employees and offer suggestions on how to fix them. Make sure they have a chance to ask questions or share their thoughts. Team members may try to divert you with another issue, but make them deal with problems. Once they understand their problems, make notes about a plan to improve their work. It is also advisable to establish a timetable for them to show improvement. Like other things in management, you need to follow up with employees. Make sure they are working on the improvement plan and remind them of the deadline, if necessary.

Each of these things can help you motivate your employees who show less initiative while keeping your more successful team members motivated. You want motivated and positive employees. Encouraging them effectively helps them find satisfaction in doing a job well and makes your job easier by automatically leading to higher productivity.

Mistakes that managers often make is treating all of their employees in the same way. I don't mean that they should favor one employee over another; what I mean is some employees need to be motivated in a different way from one of their teammates.

To effectively make a group of different personalities into a team requires a manager to get to know their team members. Too often, managers can't get results from their team because they talk to them in a harmful way. I led a team of 22 women in a home-show selling position and they were all different. Some were insecure and needed to be bolstered and given encouraging talks. Others needed lots of positive feedback to continue to do the outstanding job they were already doing.

What I found was open communication and positive feedback were the two main factors in bringing my team together and keeping them motivated. By doing that, I made my team larger and more successful. We worked as a team and we helped each other so our team could remain on top.

Sherri Smith, Author and Freelance Writer
**http://homeinsight.com/~dancer6477/wsb/index.html**

# CONCLUSION

Congratulations on your new management job. I know the feeling you had when you found out you were hired. I also know the feeling you had on your first day, when you began to get a sense of what would be expected of you.

Being a manager can be wonderful, frightening, and rewarding. I've found that each management job is a challenge in its own way. However, most management principles are the same. In this book, I focused on many of the management basics that would help you manage your responsibilities and to build a successful and lasting team.

Management does become easier with practice. The techniques and ideas in this book become easier over time. We all had that feeling in the pit of our stomachs when we started, but over time that feeling passes.

Think about the first time your team completed a rush project early or the first time your most shy employee trained someone new and they both succeeded. There will be times when your team is recognized for outstanding work. You will feel like a proud parent as the team members you hired are noticed for doing something wonderful for the company.

There are wonderful aspects to management, and I compiled this book to give you inside tips on how to succeed. I understand how difficult management can be, and I hope that sharing my successes and mistakes will help you succeed.

# RESOURCES

Albright, Mary and Clay Carr. *101 Biggest Mistakes Managers Make and How to Avoid Them.* New Jersey; Prentice Hall, 1997.

Betof, Edward and Frederic Harwood. *Just Promoted! How to Survive in Your First 12 Months as a Manager.* McGraw Hill, 1992.

Bittel, Lester R. and John W. Newstrom. *What Every Supervisor Should Know,* Sixth Edition. McGraw Hill, 1990.

Brown, W. Stephen. *13 Fatal Errors Managers Make and How You Can Avoid Them.* New York; Berkley, 1985.

Fuller, George. *The First-Time Supervisor's Survival Guide.* New York; Prentice Hall, 1995.

Fuller, George. *Supervisor's Portable Answer Book.* New Jersey, Prentice Hall, 1990.

Grossman, Jack, Ph.D. and J. Robert Parkinson, Ph.D. *Becoming a Successful Manager.* Contemporary, 2002.


www.eeoc.gov/types/sexual_harassment.html

www.eeoc.gov/policy/docs/harassment_facts.html

www.lectlaw.com/files/emp32.htm

www.eeoc.gov/policy/docs/currentissues.html

# Glossary of Terms

## A

**360-Degree Feedback** A method in which an employee may receive feedback on their own performance from their supervisor and up to eight coworkers, reporting staff members, or customers.

**Absence or Absent (Scheduled)** A period of time off from work that is previously planned during a normally scheduled work period.

**Absence or Absent (Unscheduled)** A period of time off from work during a normally scheduled work period that has not been planned.

**Absenteeism Policy** A policy that provides guidance within an organization regarding managing an employee's chronic absence from work.

**Adaptive Cultures** The environment within a company where employees, who are innovative, are encouraged, and initiative is awarded by middle- and lower-level managers.

**Attendance Policy** The expectations and guidelines for employees to report to work as written, distributed, and enforced by an organization.

# B

**Background Checking** The act of looking into a person's employment, security, or financial history before offering employment or granting a license.

**Behavioral Interview** An analysis of answers to situational questions that attempts to determine if you have the behavioral characteristics that have been selected as necessary for success in a particular job.

**Benefits** Additions to employees' base salary, such as health insurance, dental insurance, life insurance, disability insurance, a severance package, or tuition assistance.

**Bereavement Policy** The portion of an employment contract that provides for a certain amount of time off from work when an employee's spouse or close family member passes away.

**Bonus Plan** A system of rewards that generally recognizes the performance of a company's key individuals, according to a specified measure of performance.

**Bottom-Up Change** A gradual process in which the top management in a company consults with several levels of managers in the organization and develops a detailed plan for change with a timetable of events and stages the company will go through.

**Business Process** The activity of delivering goods and services to customers or promoting high quality or low costs.

**Business-Level Strategy** The strategy that a company

chooses to stress as its competitive theme.

# C

**Capabilities**  The skills a company has in coordinating its resources efficiently and productively.

**Cash Flow**  The amount of cash a business receives minus cash that must be distributed for expenses.

**Centralization**  A type of hierarchy in an organization in which upper-level managers have the authority to make the most-important decisions.

**Coaching**  A method used by managers and supervisors for providing constructive feedback to employees in order to help them continue to perform well or to identify ways in which they can improve their performance.

**Cognitive Biases**  Errors in the methods human decision makers use to process information and reach decisions.

**Commission System**
A system of rewards in which employees are paid based on how much they sell.

**Company Infrastructure**  A work environment in which all activities take place, including the organizational structure, control systems, and culture.

**Conflict Aftermath**  The long-term effects that emerge in the last stage of the conflict process.

**Counseling**  The act of providing daily feedback to employees regarding areas in which their work performance can improve.

# D

**Devil's Advocacy**  A way of improving decision making by generating a plan and a critical analysis of that plan.

**Discipline**  A process of dealing with job-related behavior that does not meet communicated performance expectations.

**Diversification** The process of entering into new industries or business areas.

**Division** The portion of a company that operates in a particular business area.

**Downsizing** The process of reducing the employee head count in an organization.

**Dress Code for Business-Casual** A company's objective to enable employees to project a professional, business-like image while experiencing the advantages of more casual and relaxed clothing.

**Employee Empowerment** The process of enabling or authorizing an individual to think, behave, take action, and control work and decision-making autonomously.

**Employee Involvement** The act of creating an environment in which people may impact decisions or actions that affect their jobs.

**Engagement** The process of involving individuals in active decision making by asking them for their input and by allowing them to refute the merits of one another's ideas and assumptions.

---

# E

**Efficiency** The measurement derived from dividing output by input.

**Empathy** The psychological characteristic that refers to understanding the feelings and viewpoints of subordinates and taking them into account when making decisions.

---

# F

**Fair Labor Standards Act (FLSA)** The legislation that requires a company to pay a non-exempt employee who works more than a 40 hour week 150 percent of their regular hourly rate for the overtime hours.

**Family and Medical Leave Act (FMLA)** The legislation which states that covered companies must grant an eligible employee up to 12 weeks of unpaid leave during any 12-month period of time for one or more of the covered reasons.

**Feedback**  The information given to or received from another person regarding the impact of their actions on a person, situation, or activity.

# G

**General Manager**  A person who bears all responsibility for the organization's overall performance or that of one of its major self-contained divisions.

**Goal**  The future state a company attempts to reach.

# H

**Human Resources**  (1) The people who are part of an organization and its operations. (2) The business function that deals with the employees of a company.

# I

**Independent Contractor**  A person or business that performs services or supplies a product for a person or business under a written or implied contract.

**Innovation**  Something that is novel or unique in the marketplace.

**Integration**  The process by which a company coordinates people and functions to accomplish certain tasks within the organization.

# M

**Marketing Strategy**  The stand a company takes regarding pricing, promotion, advertising, product design, and distribution.

**Mission Statement**  A brief but precise definition of what an organization does and why.

**Motivation**  A psychological portion of emotional intelligence that refers to a passion for work that goes beyond money or status and enables a person to pursue goals with energy and persistence.

# N

**Negativity** The concept and expression of unhappiness, anger, or frustration to other employees in the workplace.

**Networking** The act of building interpersonal relationships that could be mutually beneficial.

**New Employee Orientation** The process of orienting a new employee to a company, usually performed by one or more representatives from the Human Resources department.

**Non-Exempt Employee** Employees who are protected by the laws governing standard wages and overtime.

# O

**Optimism** The ability or tendency to look at the positive side of a situation and/or to expect the best possible results from any series of events.

**Outsourcing** The act of paying another individual or business to perform certain internal processes or functions.

# P

**Power** The capability of an individual, function, or division to cause another to do something it would not have done if left to its own devices.

**Profit-Sharing System** A system of rewards that compensates employees based on the company's profit during a specified time period.

**Progressive Discipline** A process for dealing with behavior on the job which does not meet expected and communicated performance standards.

**Project Boss** The figure of authority for a particular project.

**Promotion** The act of advancing an employee to a

position with a higher salary range maximum.

# Q

**Quality** Measurement of excellence in the desirable characteristics of a product, process, or service.

# R

**Recognition** A practice of providing attention or favorable notice to another person.

**Recruiters** People who are hired by a company to find and qualify new employees for the organization.

**Restructuring** A method of improving company performance by reducing the level of differentiation and downsizing the number of employees to decrease operating expenses.

# S

**Screening Interview** A quick, efficient discussion that is used to qualify candidates before they meet with the hiring authority.

**Self-Awareness** The psychological characteristic of a person's emotional intelligence in which he is able to understand his own moods, emotions, drives, and effect on others.

**Self-Discipline** The psychological ability to control one's own behavior.

**Sexual Harassment** The act of an employee making continued, unwelcome sexual advances, requests for sexual favors, and/or other verbal or physical conduct of a sexual nature toward another employee against her or his wishes.

**Sexual Harassment Investigation** The process of looking into an employee's complaint of sexual or other harassment in the workplace. See: Sexual Harassment.

**Social Skills** The psychological ability to interact

purposefully with others at a friendly level.

**Standardization** The level at which a business defines how decisions are to be made so that the behavior of employees becomes predictable.

**Strategic Alliances** Cooperative agreements between companies that are sometimes also competitors.

**Strategy** The actions a person or company takes to achieve one or more of its goals or superior performance.

**Values** Traits or characteristics that are considered to be worthwhile and that represent an individual's priorities and driving forces.

**Vision** Also called a Mission. A statement of the goals that the company would like to achieve over the medium- to long-term.

# T

**Trust - Interpersonal and Organizational** The condition in which a person or business is ready to interact with someone or something without walls or hesitation.

# V

**Validate** To check a policy set for potential problems in the event that the policy set becomes active.

# INDEX

## ABOUT THE AUTHOR

Shri Henkel is from the Shenandoah Valley of Virginia. She had a strong desire to create and write for many years. Shri owns a management and marketing consulting business and is a freelance writer and marketing professional.

Her first three non-fiction books, which focus on business management, will be released in 2006. The first is a guide for first-time managers, the second is specifically targeted to pizza and sub shop managers or owners. Each will be available from Atlantic Publishing.

Shri has 21 years of business management experience and 15 years of marketing experience. She uses the knowledge she gained in this work to create a helpful guidebook for business managers. These experiences include things that work and tips about things to avoid.

Shri worked as an assistant manager, marketing coordinator, and then a store manger for Domino's Pizza. This experience was invaluable when writing the pizza and sub shop book.

In addition to her non-fiction work, Shri has two novels that were released in early 2006. Her love of the coast, history, and lighthouses shows in her stories. On a trip to Cape Ann with her brother Chris, Shri discovered the area that is the setting for a series of books. The rugged land, hard-working people, and rich history were too compelling to ignore. Cape Ann and Gloucester, Massachusetts, are the setting for several of her books that focus on the "Stormy View" lighthouse.

For more information about Shri's work, visit her fiction Web site at **www.nikkileigh.com** or her business Web site at **www.sandcconsulting.com**.